THE EMPTY MEADOW

Stanton & Lee Publishers, Inc.

THE EMPTY MEADOW

Ben Logan

Illustrations by Marian Lefebvre

The Empty Meadow is fiction. Though the time and place are real,
the characters and events are creations of the imagination.

First Edition
Copyright © 1983 by Ben Logan.
All rights reserved.
Illustration Copyright © 1983 by Marian Lefebvre.
All rights reserved.
Direct all inquiries to:
Stanton & Lee Publishers, Inc.
44 East Mifflin Street On the Square
Madison, Wisconsin 53703

Library of Congress Cataloging in Publication Data
Logan, Ben, 1920—
  The empty meadow.
  I. Title.
PS3562.0'444E46   1982   813'.54   82-17060
ISBN 0-88361-087-6

for Jacqueline

A voice was calling me, lifting me up from the covers that were heavy because it was only May and nights were still cool. The voice was pulling me away from a night filled with dreams where I was both child and adult and I kept starting on some wonderous new journey that forever just took me back to being a child again, still locked away on the hilltop world of the farm.

I could feel the sun warm on my face and when I opened my eyes, it was filling the little bedroom with orange gold. Mom was standing in the doorway, looking amused, her hair loose like a young girl's, not yet gathered into the neat bun that would change her into a woman for the rest of the day.

"Know what you said just before you woke up?"

I shook my head.

"You said 'bird's nest. It's a new bird's nest!' "

"I did? I don't know why I would have said that."

I remembered part of the dream, but it wasn't about a bird's nest. I had been somewhere down in the valley, along the creek, with whippoor-wills calling from the hillside and a darkhaired girl running ahead of me at the edge of the stream, looking back over her shoulder at me and laughing. The sand was warm under my feet, the smell of mint in the air and no matter how fast I ran she was always a little ahead of me, the wind lifting her hair. I tried to pull the girl in the dream back, but she was slipping away from me in the morning sunlight just as she had in the dream.

"Are you really awake?" Mom said.

I remembered my plans for the day and quit trying to find the dream. "I'm practically up," I said.

She left me. I heard her calling my brothers. Then her footsteps went on to the kitchen. There was the sound of the outside door opening and I knew what was happening. She would be standing on the porch, listening to the birds and looking around her at the new morning.

From the lane behind the house I could hear Dad calling the cows. "Come Boss. Come Boss."

I got dressed and went out through the window so I wouldn't disturb Mom. The sun was breaking up into bright-colored prisms of light on the dew. A little breeze stirred the top branches of the big soft maple tree in the front yard. The oatfields were smooth carpets of bright, bright green.

Still poking in my shirttail I went around the house and found Dad standing at the milkcan rack, looking down at the bank of fog that filled the valley leading up from the Kickapoo River. Something about it reminded him of his childhood in Norway.

I went on past him without speaking. The last of the cows had come up the lane and were bunched close to the gate, tails flipping at the flies. I let them through and headed them into the barn.

Dad was still at the milkcan rack. I rattled a milkpail and he smiled at me, but he was frowning. He looked up at the windmill to check the direction of the wind, looked to our own fields on our own narrow ridge, looked to the horizon where other ridges were beginning to show through the morning haze. He shook his head.

"What's the matter?"

"Funny year," he said. "Haven't even got the corn planted and it feels like July. Going to be a real scorcher. Summer's coming too fast, like it's fixing to be hot and dry."

My brothers came out of the house. Lars was five years older and had almost blond hair, a lot like mine. Erik, who was only three years older, had dark hair and he was always different. They both looked sleepy because they'd been out the night before playing cards. I watched them, trying to see inside them. Did they ever have those kinds of dreams, with a girl running ahead of them, not sure if they were more afraid they would catch her or that she would get away?

2

It was only ten o'clock, but the sun was already high and hot when my brothers let me out of the car in Gordon's Landing. The street was soft under my feet and the smell of tar came up. It was the way a hot Sunday morning should feel in town, promising things that couldn't happen in a million years in the hay and pasture smells of the farm, way up on the ridge.

Lars and Erik looked out at me, the way Dad might have, reminding me that there was no way to keep older brothers from being partly parents.

"You sure you're going to be all right here all day?" Lars said.

"I'll be all right."

"Well don't forget. You get in trouble, we get in trouble."

We'd made this deal. I wouldn't tag along with them all day and they wouldn't tell that I'd stopped off all day in Gordon's Landing.

"See you about six this afternoon," Erik said. He winked. "Take it easy. Lots of girls in this town."

"Sure."

They were both grinning. I could feel my face getting hot. I had just turned seventeen, and they didn't think I was old enough to get into that kind of trouble. I wasn't sure I was either.

They pulled out, heading up-river to a place where they wanted to try the fishing. Maybe try a few other things, too. The car left little ruts in the hot tar as it went down to the end of the street and turned right, onto the river road.

A man in a red sweat shirt was loading a truck down the street at the fish house. I was supposed to meet Billy Wallin. His place was across the street, an old yellow house with his family's filling station and store in front. I couldn't see anybody around and the brass padlocks were still on the gaspumps.

The man at the fish house slammed the door of the truck and pulled away, water from the melting ice spilling out at the back each time he changed gears. The truck turned down-river which meant it was going south, maybe clear to Chicago.

Just for a minute I could hear an organ and singing, and I realized it was only when a little wind blew down the hollow from the ridges up above that the sound from the church carried into the lower part of town.

The filling station door squeaked open and an old man came out. He was thin and tall, had on long underwear and was hooking his suspenders up over his shoulders and carrying a pair of shoes. He eased himself into a chair next to the gaspumps, started scratching himself through the underwear and looking out over the river and then up to the bluffs. When he had his shoes on, he unlocked the padlocks and started raising gas up into the glass tanks at the top of the old fashioned pumps, pulling the handles back and forth, one in each hand, the gas bubbling up, orange in one tank, purple in the other.

I walked across the street, feeling the hot air pushing against my face. The old man finished pumping and looked at me, but he didn't say anything. I'd never seen anybody before with such deep-set eyes and so many lines in his face.

"Billy around?"

"Not unless he fell out of bed, woke himself up by mistake."

His voice sounded young, so much like Billy's that I jumped.

The screendoor made its squeak.

"He's getting dressed." Billy's sister, Eva Mae, was standing in the open door, wearing thin pajamas that were pulled down low in front. She was licking away on a strawberry ice cream cone. She was about fifteen and seemed different than she had the one other time I had seen her. My face started feeling hot from the way she licked at the cone and looked at me. Finally she did a lazy turn back through the door, her bottoms round against the pajamas. When I looked up from following her out of sight, the old man was right beside me. He winked and started laughing. There were tobacco stains all over his teeth.

"Think she'd make a good first one, do you, Boy?"

I noticed the smell of gasoline. I shifted from one foot to the other trying to think of some way to change the subject.

"How old are you, Boy?"

"Seventeen."

"My God!" He shook his head. "You know how long it's been since I was seventeen?"

"Quite awhile I guess."

"Eighty years! That's what it's been since I was seventeen."

I backed away. "Would you please tell Billy I'm over at the fish house?"

He just took a deep breath and held it, smiling a little, standing perfectly motionless, shoulders straight, head back and each hand holding onto a bottle of oil.

I went across the street and sat down on the loading dock where water was spreading in little circles from ice that had spilled out of the fish boxes. Sweat was running under my shirt. All at once I felt out of place in the hot, motionless day. Up on the ridge, chances were the wind would be blowing and air moving around you. In the valley, it was all held in by the hills. Even the river seemed to be just passing through, coming from someplace, going someplace, but not stopping to be part of anything here.

The old man was still standing exactly the same way at the gaspumps. What had happened over there kept flipping into my head and I kept flipping it away. For a moment I had a good notion to start walking home. That was how it had been lately. Something I wasn't ready for would suddenly be there and all I seemed to know how to do was push it right down again and run away.

The door of the station squeaked. Billy came out buttoning up his shirt and carrying three ice cream cones in a cardboard holder. He took one of the bottles of oil out of the old man's hand and gave him a cone. Then he came across the street and gave me one, four scoops high, each a different flavor. The old man was still looking out over the river, every now and then taking a lick of the ice cream.

"Who's that?" I said.

Billy grinned. "That's the Oldest Man in the World."

"No he isn't."

"He is," Billy said. "He's past ninety-six."

"He doesn't look that old."

"Well he is. His name's Bill Wallin, same as mine. He's my great-grandfather."

I stared at Billy. We were in high school together, but I didn't know him very well and he was always springing things on me.

"Sure he is," Billy said. "He lives with us."

The old man started moving, setting out more bottles of oil with one hand.

"How about that?" Billy said. "The Oldest Man in the World licking an ice cream cone."

I still wasn't sure. "What about your great-grandmother?"

"Hell, I guess she's been dead forever."

For quite awhile we sat in the hot tar and fish smell, waving flies away and working at the sweet, smooth ice cream.

"What you want to do?" Billy said.

"You know. Ride the train."

"Just an old train."

"Sure, for you. I never hitched a ride before."

"OK," he said. "Be awhile."

Billy picked up a piece of ice and squeezed it, water leaking out between his fingers. A car went through town, cane fishpoles tied to the hood ornament and curved back over the roof to the rear bumper. For a minute there was a little air moving around us.

"Even cars sound different on Sunday," I said.

Billy was gritting his teeth, watching the water come out of his fist. Finally the dripping stopped. He worked his fingers and took a deep breath. "That damn ice sure is cold."

All at once I heard the train coming from down-river and I jumped off the dock.

"Take it easy," Billy said. "Not even close yet."

I sat down again, right where Billy had been letting the cold water drip and he laughed at me. The train was getting louder. It gave a long whistle.

"Seven, eight minutes yet," Billy said.

The door slammed across the street. Billy's sister came over with three more ice cream cones, gave us each one and stood about a foot away, staring at Billy.

"No," Billy said.

"Why not?"

"Because I said so."

She came over and stared at me the same way. She was a funny looking girl, not very tall, with a roundish face and her hair cut a way that made it stick out around her face. Her eyes were funny, too, big and dark. After she'd stared at me for a minute, that was the only part of her I could see.

"Tell her no," Billy said.

I had to stop looking at the eyes. Her tongue was going back and forth along the top of the cone, curling up on the return lick to pull the melting ice cream into her mouth. We kept looking at each other, both licking away and I felt ten years old, and in kneepants with summer dust squeezing up between my toes.

Eva Mae pushed the ice cream down into the cone with her tongue. "I could sneak us some food."

Billy looked at me.

"No more ice cream," I said.

"Two pound box of soda crackers and a ring of baloney," Billy said.

She smiled. Her whole face changed and she wasn't so funny-looking anymore. She stuffed the rest of the cone into her mouth and ran back across the street.

The train whistled for the crossing just below town. We watched the door of the station. In a minute she came out, holding a paper bag close in front of her. The old man said something. She put a finger up to her lips and ran toward the tracks.

"Come on!" Billy said.

We caught up with Eva Mae at the intersection. The train roared in as we slid down the bank. There was dust all around us. Half the dogs in town were barking.

The train was going slower. Dust settled down. I could feel it between my teeth.

"Got to get on the other side," Billy yelled.

I looked over my shoulder and Eva Mae was right behind us, the paper bag swinging in her hand. Way back at the filling station, the old man was watching.

We ran with the train, sparks shooting out from behind the wheels, so close I could feel the heat. We cut across the tracks right in front of the engine and scooted into the weeds. The engine went by with the wheels grinding against the rails.

"Stay down," Billy yelled.

We flopped on our bellies, the ground shaking us up and down. Eva Mae was in the middle and I could feel some part of her touching me each time she breathed.

I grabbed Billy's arm and pointed to a boxcar with an open door. He shook his head. The train was moving very slowly, a loose rail rising and falling as the wheels rolled over it.

The engine stopped. Each car crashed into the next one, the crashes moving back along the train even after the cars in front of us had stopped.

All at once it was still except for the dogs. I reached across Eva Mae and poked Billy.

"When it starts up again," he said.

Dust settled on us and sweat was tickling under my shirt.

"Down flat!" Billy whispered.

A man in striped overalls was walking toward us in the loose gravel, checking the door of each car. I could hear Eva Mae breathing. We put our faces down tight against the ground and the footsteps went on by.

"Get ready," Billy said.

The train jerked ahead, hitches clanging one after another down the line. Billy crawled on his hands and knees toward the track. We followed. At the edge of the weeds we all crowded together. Eva Mae's shoulder pushed into my side and her hair had a sunburned smell.

"Come on!" Billy said and he ran toward a boxcar, crouching low and zig-zagging like somebody in a war movie. He slid the door open and hopped up. I flopped into the doorway on my belly and wiggled there, legs dangling down toward the wheels.

The train was speeding up. By the time I got turned around, Billy was pulling Eva Mae in. She still had the paper bag. Billy slid the door shut and we stumbled back to the rear of the car and sat down in a corner, Eva Mae between us, bracing ourselves against the swaying. I couldn't see anything in the darkness except dust floating up in the little needles of sunshine that came through cracks around the door.

The wheels banged over the rail joints, bouncing us up and down on the wooden floor, then became a steady clicking. The bell at the crossing above town began to ding, getting louder, then fading behind us.

I began to get used to the darkness. Eva Mae's eyes seemed as big as baseballs. Billy slouched away from us and got up. With his legs spread far apart, he walked to the door and pushed it open. I stayed where I was with Eva Mae's shoulder pressed against me. Outside, the telegraph poles flipped by, seeming to move much faster than the solid green of the brush and trees, farther back.

All at once the sound changed, the green disappeared and there was the open water of the river, reaching all the way across to the Iowa side, two or three miles away.

Eva Mae leaned forward to see and her hair brushed against my face. I wanted to get up and go over to the door with Billy, but I stayed with her.

The river kept sliding by downstream while we went upstream. A man fishing from a rowboat waved and Billy's arm swept across the open door.

The train eased into a turn. The pull carried me away from Eva Mae. A little island slid into place in the doorway, an old houseboat beached on the sandy shore, smoke coming up from the crooked stovepipe with its funny dunce cap on the top. As we swung out of the curve, the island moved to the rear of the door and was gone. My shoulder came back against Eva Mae.

"Don't break the crackers," she said.

Vibration made the dust and chaff on the floor bounce and gather into little moving circles. We still hadn't picked up much speed. Billy leaned out the door and shook his head.

The train whistled and began to slow, the wheels clattering. Eva Mae's shoulder kept banging into my side and she was staring at me, all eyes again.

Billy came back from the door. His lips moved, but I couldn't hear anything. He realized he'd been trying to whisper and he yelled "They must be stopping at the work siding. We got to be ready to get off."

The wheels grabbed onto the rails. From up ahead, the banging of closing couplings moved toward us. Billy made us stay back from the door. Our car crashed into the next one ahead.

"Come on!" Billy whispered.

I jumped out. It was so quiet I could feel the whole train crew watching. When I turned around to help Eva Mae, she fell right on top of me and we both went rolling. Billy went full speed out through the door, hit the ground running and headed for the brush, zig-zagging, grasshoppers taking off ahead of him like ricochetting bullets. I pulled Eva Mae up and when we caught up, Billy was behind a clump of brush, stretched out flat on his back, chewing on a piece of grass. "What kept you?" he asked.

Eva Mae giggled. "We ran into each other."

Billy laughed, then grabbed my arm and pulled me down. The same striped-overalls man walked up to the car where we'd been. He checked inside, slid the door shut, and looked all around, his eyes stopping once on the bushes where we were. Finally, he walked on toward the rear of the train.

The day was different now, the ground solid and unmoving under us, the sun cooking down. A big dusthopper went rattling off and I jumped at the dry, brittle sound.

The train jerked back the way we'd come, running the last car onto the siding, a flatcar loaded with new ties. They were black and dripping in the hot sun and I could smell the sharp fumes of the creosote. The men unhooked the flatcar and left it. The train clattered ahead. When the caboose came by, we could see a window box on the back filled with bright red petunias that looked perfectly happy riding along in the hot sun.

Billy laughed. "Those are Smitty's. They call him Smitty flower seed." Billy pointed to the hollyhock plants close to the tracks. "He planted those, too."

The caboose went out of sight around the curve, leaving us alone with the soft grass and the hot day that didn't have anything to do with trains.

We skirted along the edge of the slough and crawled up the bank to the blacktop. Beyond the road, the hillside sloped up steeply to the top of the rocky bluffs, five or six hundred feet above the river. A small stream ran out of a narrow ravine into the slough. Eva Mae kept stopping to look up at the bluffs.

Billy led the way into the woods. A breeze was coming from somewhere farther up the ravine and the place smelled of flowers, dampness and dust. We reached a little clearing with a tin-roofed shack that was half fallen. Close by was the spring where the stream began. Billy and I pushed the watercress out of the way and drank with our faces buried in the cold water. We were sprawled under the trees half asleep by the time

Eva Mae caught up. She dropped the food bag and went on up the hillside, out of sight. A few minutes later we heard rocks rolling and a bluejay scolding. Billy sat up. "Aw, she's got nine lives," he said, slumping down again.

"What's she doing up there?"

"Who knows what a sister's doing?" Billy pointed up at the bluffs. "See that little pinnacle of rock? Well Great-Gramps says some Indian princess jumped from up there once. Because her father wouldn't let her marry who she wanted to. People call it Lover's Leap."

The leaping rock was about four feet out from the edge of the bluff. It was only about four feet square. Finally Eva Mae was there, standing right at the drop-off, looking out at the other rock. All at once she jumped across the opening. It seemed like a long time before she landed on her hands and knees on the little pinnacle.

Billy flopped back to the ground. "Don't worry about her. She drives you crazy if you let her see you worrying about her."

"She can't tell we're looking at her from way down here."

"She knows all right."

He turned his back and started whittling a sharp point on a long stick. Eva Mae was standing up now, leaning forward into the wind, like a fancy radiator ornament on an old car or one of those pictures of a pioneer woman looking toward the horizon out on the western prairies. I could see her skirt blowing against her.

Billy rolled over and speared the food bag with his stick. Using his pocket knife, he cut the baloney up into little circles, putting each one between two cracker squares. The meat was salty and spicey and I forgot about Eva Mae for a while. When I looked up again, the rock was empty.

We went on eating and pretty soon she was there with us. I handed her some food. Her blouse was wet and sticking to her. She didn't seem so young now. Once I'd noticed, I couldn't stop looking.

Billy found a rusty tin can, dipped water from the spring and passed it around. The roar of a train came in to us, the bright silver of the passenger cars flashing through the trees. After it was gone, a deep whistle blew out on the river. Billy walked to the mouth of the ravine. He was smiling when he came back. "River boat," he said. "Headed north. Damn thing's probably going all the way up to the Twin Cities."

He sat down, still smiling, poking at the green moss with his stick.

Eva Mae was looking at me. She had unbuttoned the top of her blouse and the V was showing. Billy was right there, a few feet away, poking away with his stick, not paying any attention. I thought she was going to move closer and I got up. "Let's do something," I said.

We took a last drink from the spring, Eva Mae leaning way back while she drank from the tin can and she was sticking out at the world again. She caught me staring and laughed.

We went back across the road to the tracks. It was cooler there, even out in the strong sun, because a little wind was blowing off the river.

For quite awhile we just sat and looked at that big stretch of water, almost three miles wide, riding past us, a world all its own. A couple of times a fish rolled at the edge of the rocks.

We began walking south, towards Gordon's Landing, Billy straggling behind in one of his sleepy moods, arms swinging loose, feet plowing along in the gravel. Eva Mae came up beside me, matching her steps to mine, skipping every other tie. Her blouse had dried out. The wind was pushing it against her.

All at once, Eva Mae ran ahead and knelt in the weeds along the track. She held out a small, dark red strawberry. It was sweet tasting but sharp at the same time. I sucked at it and she looked up with a pleased smile like a silly old mother hen that's found a goodie for her chicks.

Billy caught up.

I pointed. "Strawberries."

"Sure," he said, "figured on that."

The patch of wild berries ran for a quarter of a mile or more on both sides of the tracks. We picked hundreds and ate as we walked.

Billy fell behind again. I sat down on one of the rails and sorted through the rounded river gravel. Eva Mae stopped right behind me with her leg touching my shoulder. I picked up a stone about the size of a chicken egg, smooth and warm from the sun. Her leg moved against my back and I got up. I still had the stone in my hand. I looked away from her and saw the blue insulator on the telegraph pole. It was smooth and perfect sticking up from the crossbar and I threw without thinking about it. The blue fell to pieces. The wire jerked and hummed. Broken glass tinkled down, flashing in the sun, falling through the hollyhocks onto the rocks below, pieces bouncing and landing in the slough, ripples spreading on the brown water.

Eva Mae touched my arm. She gave me another stone and it was warm in my hand.

From behind us there was a sharp crack, the sound of the wire jerking and glass falling. Billy was picking up another stone. I threw the one I was holding. It missed and arced out into the water. Eva Mae handed me another and we went down the track, throwing and throwing.

I started skipping every other pole so Billy could do that one, and we moved toward Gordon's Landing breaking the bright blue of the insulators as we went.

A train roared by from the south, shaking the ground. The engineer yelled something at us. There was a hobo riding in the open door of a boxcar, legs dangling out. "Give 'em hell, Boys!" he yelled. "Give 'em holy hell!"

Eva Mae seemed to be standing closer each time. When I threw, my shoulder would touch her and she'd laugh and lean down to get another stone. Finally my arm was so tired I was missing almost every time. Billy quit and sprawled out on his back in the weeds, a couple of poles back. I turned to Eva Mae and didn't know what I was going to do. She moved past me and began running along one of the rails. I tried running after her on the opposite rail, but I wasn't used to it. She waited and when I caught up, reached out her hand, still standing on the other rail, and we walked that way, our hands together.

Eva Mae could walk without looking down the way I had to do. Her face was twisted up as though there was something she was trying to say. I watched my feet on the shiny steel and they were somebody else's feet and I was over between the tracks where our hands were touching.

We walked that way for a long time before the train whistle came from behind us. Her face had that big, glued-on smile again.

The rails began to shake and I knew the train must be on our track. She glanced at me. I thought she was waiting for me to look back, so I didn't. The shaking got stronger. The whistle was blowing in short blasts. The roar of the engine seemed right on top of us. Her hand gave mine a squeeze and let go. She went one way. I went the other. The train was between us.

It was a long train. My chest was pressed down into the warm gravel. Even with the ground shaking, I could feel my heart pounding. The wheels were banging across a rail joint just two feet away and pretty soon it was the only sound left in the world.

I raised up a little and could see Eva Mae. She was staring under the cars, her face all eyes, hand raised as though she was about to reach into the wheels.

The ground stopped shaking. A little whirl of wind ran down the track after the train, picking up the dust. I could feel the hot sun baking down on my wet shirt. From the edge of the slough, a red-winged blackbird was scolding.

Eva Mae was staring across the rail, her hand reaching toward a tiny violet growing out of a crack in the wooden tie. The blossom was still swaying back and forth in the wind from the train.

Billy flopped down in the gravel beside me, breathing hard. He mopped sweat off his face with his shirttail and hit me on the arm. "You're sure not letting her see you worry about her," he said.

I grinned and hit him back. It was the first time he'd ever made me feel an equal in his valley world. Eva Mae started laughing. The laugh got higher and higher, then stopped right in the middle. My knees were shaking when I got up. We started toward Gordon's Landing again, Billy behind, Eva Mae and I walking on the rails, not touching and not looking at each other. The warmth came up from the gravel and all I could see was the shiny steel under my feet.

The air was cooler all at once and I realized the sun wasn't baking straight down on us anymore. It was coming from across the river, making a bright blaze on the water.

A river boat whistled, humming upstream with its line-up of barges. Billy slouched against a telegraph pole, watching the boat.

Eva Mae reached for my hand and we kept walking, her fingers digging into my palm. Near the train station, she pulled me off the tracks, over to the wooden water tower and showed me how to cup my hands under a leak and catch enough to sip.

The air was cool under the tower. The water made little puddles in the powdery dust and the smell was like the first few minutes of a summer rain. Mud dauber wasps were rolling up little balls of the mud, thrashing the air as they tried to take off.

I remembered I hadn't seen Billy for a long time. I looked around for him and Eva Mae giggled and pointed. He was way back, leaning against the same pole, looking out where the boat and barges had been.

Eva Mae pulled her skirt up and got down on her knees under the tower, making roads in the mud. After a minute I got down with her. We built hills, streams and dams, waving the mud daubers away until she got the idea of letting them have one flat place for an airfield.

Somebody laughed. A man was walking by, looking at us, carrying a lunch bucket in one hand, a bottle of beer in the other. I got up and washed my hands off in one of the dripping places. Eva Mae joined me, her hands touching mine in the water. She was starting to get the look again that made her whole face into nothing but eyes. Billy was still back along the tracks in exactly the same position.

Just beyond the water tower, an open lot sloped down to a dock where river boats tied up sometimes. We walked that way and sat down on an old rowboat, watching the sun go lower. The light and colors kept changing, deep shadows almost hiding our side of the islands while the sun still shone in our eyes. The jukebox at the tavern was playing. Out on the river, a fisherman in a big flat-bottomed rowboat was pulling in nets, singing the same song over and over.

Eva Mae moved up closer. The sun dropped almost to the hills on the Iowa side. A few shadflies flew past us, rising off the river, heading in to find the lights. A train was rumbling, coming from down-river.

I knew I had to go pretty soon because my brothers would be coming back. I moved a little and could feel Eva Mae against me. There was an old shed halfway between the river and the street. We got up and walked through the weeds and, without either of us saying anything, went through the door that was hanging by one hinge.

For a minute I couldn't even see her, but I could hear her breathing. The train was closer. She moved and I could hear the sound her clothes made. I reached for her, but I didn't know where I dared touch her. I just put my hands on her shoulders. She was shaking. Her head dropped. "I don't know how to do anything," she said.

The train whistled. We stood that way and let it roar past, the little shed shaking, dust coming down, the door swinging on the top hinge.

The train went on through without stopping. We walked out of the shed and she had that big smile again by the time we reached the filling station.

"Anytime you want to break those blue glass things, you come see me," she said. She squeezed my hand, then ran inside, the screendoor banging behind her.

A sound came from the deep shadows at the end of the porch. The old man was there, his chair teetered back against the wall, and he was nodding as though he'd seen everything that had happened all day. He straightened up until part of his face was in the light. For the first time he looked like the Oldest Man in the World. I backed away, but he leaned forward, following me without ever getting up from the chair.

"Well?" he said.

I shook my head.

He laughed, his eyes getting bigger, like Eva Mae's. "Plenty of time yet."

He stopped laughing and looked right through me. "Great God-almighty! Eighty years!"

Finally I was able to turn around and walk down toward the tavern where my brothers would be waiting to take me back up to the ridge.

3

A week later, Billy and I were hanging around the station on Saturday night. Billy's great-grandfather — everybody was calling him either Bill or Old Bill — was out front with five other men, all of them teetered against the wall in their round-back chairs, swatting at bugs that flapped around the gaspumps. Billy said we'd hear better stories if we stayed out of plain sight. That was all right with me because I didn't want the old man bringing up anything about Eva Mae.

An old man the others called Charlie kept looking around at the dry dusty evening that didn't have any feel of dampness in it. Finally he started shaking his head. "I tell you, boys, there's no use planting any more crops this year. Saw a summer start out like this back in nineteen-aught-eight. We went. . . ."

"It was 1909," another man said.

"No it wasn't," Charlie said. "It was nineteen-aught-eight. Same year we lost three horses with the sleeping sickness."

"All right. All right, get on with it," the other man said.

"Perfectly willing to discuss it," Charlie said. "But it was aught-eight. Like I started to say, we went sixty-seven days that summer without any rain. Wasn't a bit of corn that fall. Not even nubbins. This year's looking up to be just like that."

Billy's great grandfather looked at the other men and smiled a little. "Say, Charlie, how's that new neighbor doing?"

"I won't say a word about him."

Everyone waited.

"All right," Charlie said, "I will say this. That son of a bitch is no good."

"What makes you say that?"

Charlie shook his head. "Won't say another word."

"Come on, Charlie."

Billy started giggling, trying to cover it up with his hands.

"What's going on?" I whispered. Billy shook his head.

"Yeah, Charlie," one of the men said. "Come on."

"Well, all right. That son of a bitch ain't got a wife, you know. Couple times lately he's been sniffing around at my daughter."

Billy nudged me and whispered. "His daughter's close to fifty and ain't had anything but overalls on for about twenty-nine."

"Won't say another word. Well, I will say this. You can tell him I said so, too. That son of a bitch better keep away from her or he won't need any buttons on the front of his pants anymore."

"How come?"

"Because there won't be anything left in there to hang out, that's why!"

Old Bill got his chair down on all four legs long enough to scratch a match and get his pipe going. "I ever tell you about the time I used to raise hounds? Had eighteen of 'em once. Thirteen bitches. God, when two-three got in heat at the same time be male dogs from clean across the county hanging around. Finally figured out just one thing to do when you got a bitch in heat and don't want any more pups."

He stopped talking and puffed hard on his pipe a few times.

"What's that, Bill?" one of the men said.

"Lock her up!"

"Makes sense to me all right."

Everybody was looking at Charlie. He was staring off into the dark where the lightning bugs were flashing. He shook his head. "No, Sir. No rain. You could walk straight out there for a thousand miles and wouldn't find rain. Not even going to be any dew."

He pulled out his watch and snapped the case open, holding it up so the light from the gaspump would shine on it. "About that time." He walked down into the street. In a minute an old pickup truck started up and went chugging out of town.

The men watched him go.

"Think he heard what I was saying?" Old Bill said.

"About time he heard it from somebody. If that guy's been going over to see her, he's just saving her the trip."

"Hell, Charlie don't hear anything he don't want to. Take that year there wasn't any corn. That was 1909, same summer Buckshot Evans lost his arm in the threshing machine."

Across the river to the west the light was gone from the sky except for a little color close over the Iowa hills. Crickets were calling and frogs were croaking down in the slough even if it was half dried-up.

The screendoor opened and closed very slowly. Eva Mae slipped in between Billy and me.

"You're not supposed to be out here when the men're talking," Billy whispered.

She stuck out her tongue at him and crowded up closer to me. Her bare leg was pressing against my leg and was dancing up and down.

A car full of kids a little older than Billy and I came tearing down the street, a head sticking out of every window. It roared into the intersection where the main street dead-ended into the river road, then squealed around in a tight U-turn.

One of the men snorted. "By God, those fool kids are just no good nowdays — tearing around the country ass-over-appetite."

"Don't know as I'd put it that way," Old Bill said. "But by God this country is some different all right. Bottoms used to be so thick with timber you had to turn sideways to walk between trees. I remember my grandfather coming in day after day with a wagon load of fish. Train used to stop here special to load up on passenger pigeons the hunters shot for the Chicago market. God-almighty, those pigeons blacked out the sun for days at a time in the fall. All gone now. How the hell could there be that many and now they're all gone?"

A younger man had been leaning against one of the gaspumps. "Guess there's not much mystery about that, Bill. You already told us. Wagon loads of fish. Train load of passenger pigeons. What do you expect?"

The man turned and walked away.

"Who the hell's that?"

"New game warden," Old Bill said. "Could be right, too. About the pigeons, I mean."

"Say, where was you born, Bill?" a man asked.

"Don't know for sure. Somewhere on the trail coming up from Ohio is the way it was told to me. My mother died before we got here. My father was never one to write anything down. It was sometime in the summer of 1842. Wasn't hardly anybody around here then they say."

"My God, 1842! That's almost a hundred years ago. You that old?"

"I guess I must be."

"Didn't you shoot a buffalo once, Bill?"

"Nope. Had a chance one time when I was just a kid. Out on Elm Tree Island. Figure he was the last one and was out there all by himself. I had a rifle with me — seems like it was a .25-20. This bunch of wolves, four of 'em, had him circled. God he was big. They'd tore him up some. There was blood on the snow. Them wolves must've been starving. I started shooting and they didn't even run off. I got all four of 'em."

"What about the buffalo?"

"Well, that was a funny thing. He stood there looking at me like he was hoping I'd shoot him too. Then he headed across the ice to the Iowa side."

"How old was you then?"

"Must've been around twelve I think."

"That would've made it 1854. I thought the buffalo was all gone by then."

"So did everybody else," Old Bill said. "Figure he was the last one ever got this close to the Wisconsin side of the river."

Billy was nodding. "They always try to trap him. They never do though."

Down at the intersection the car went around in a circle for maybe the twentieth time. "Damn fool kids," one of the men said.

"Not like when you were young, huh Bill?" The man winked at the others.

Old Bill teetered back. "Damn right it's not. Hell, I was seventy years old before I ever rode in a car. But there was things could be done in a buggy. A whole hell of a lot you could do with a girl while a horse went down the road without any help from you."

There was laughing all at once from down at the intersection as the car drove in a tight circle around a girl.

Bill watched the car a minute. Then he laughed and whacked his leg. "I ever tell you about the time I had this new girl and the horse didn't know the way to take her home? Well I was pretty busy. That sure wasn't the first time she'd been in a buggy. After while the horse stopped and I could hear him eating. Didn't pay no attention. Figured he was eating weeds along the road. Like I said, I was busy."

Eva Mae's leg danced a little jig against mine. She was leaning over, her chin in her hands, like somebody listening to a Mother Goose story.

"And by God, just as I was getting the busiest of all, this real polite voice said, 'Pardon me.'

"Well I raised up and here's this fool man standing there in a long nightgown, holding up a lantern. You know where we were? Right square in the middle of this Goddamned garden.

" 'Pardon me,' the guy said again. 'I hate to disturb you, but would you mind getting your horse and buggy out of my flowerbed?' "

Old Bill leaned back and laughed until tears ran down his face. The other men teetered back and forth in their chairs laughing with him.

Finally the old man wiped his eyes with a big red handkerchief. "Well, Sir. We went galloping out of there. The moon was down and I couldn't see a damn thing. To this day I don't know where the hell that flowerbed was or who that 'Pardon me' guy was."

"You go home then, Bill?"

"Started to. Figured she'd be all spooked up, but turned out she was laughing, not crying. 'Bill,' she said. 'The least you could've done was pick me some posies.' So I let the horse take over and I got busy again."

The men laughed. "What ever happened to that girl, Bill?"

He stopped laughing. "Damned if I know. Guess I let her get away. Hell, I was always losing one girl back then while I was chasing me another one. She was a good spunky one, too. Name was Ellie. That's it, Ellie. Get to thinking sometimes that was the name of one lived up on Sand Creek. But God, that one was ten times the girl Ellie was, so why'n hell can't I remember her name?"

He sat and rocked on the back legs of his chair and looked out to where the moon was starting to shine on the river.

Billy had been leaning back, his shoulder against mine. Suddenly he sat up straight. "Jesus Christ!" he said. "Jesus H. Christ!" He was whispering but his voice was rough and he was shaking his head.

"What's the matter?" I asked.

He glared at me. "Not a Goddamned thing you'd understand!"

Eva Mae was staring at him.

"Hey," one of the men said, "remember that Johnson girl used to wait tables down to French Prairie? Asked her for an ash tray once. She came back, a plate of food in each hand, the ash tray sitting level as a pool table on her you-know-what's. 'Grab the one in the middle,' she said."

"I remember her," another man said. "She'd been chased up the wainscoting a few times. She was a good runner, but she got caught up with pretty often."

"Course she did," the first man said. "Way she liked it, too. There's some fall off the tree like a ripe plum. Some you got to chase to hell and gone before she lets happen what she knows is going to happen all the time. Either way, ain't that what girls are for?"

I waited for the other men to laugh. No one did. I didn't understand why they laughed at Old Bill's talk and didn't laugh at this man. I looked at Eva Mae, remembered last Sunday in the shed down by the river, and wondered which kind the man would say she was.

The car had stopped in the intersection. One boy was hanging out the window talking to the girl in the street and we could hear them laughing. The door opened, the girl crawled in and the car roared up the river road, tires squealing, leaving a big cloud of dust hanging. When the smell of it reached us, Old Bill looked up and shook his head. "Damn country's getting churned up into nothing but dust."

Eva Mae was pushing against me and staring with that big-eyed look.

"Pardon me," Billy said. "I hate to disturb you, but how about walking down to the river?"

I slid away from Eva Mae. She slipped inside without anyone seeing her. Billy and I walked down the dusty street. The moon had come up above the hills and the river was bright up ahead. A little wind was coming off the water and the only place it felt cool was where Eva Mae had been leaning against me.

"Hey," I said, "does Eva Mae do everybody like that?"

"Do what?"

"You know. Push up against them like that."

"Never noticed."

"Well, does she know what she's doing? I mean does she do it on purpose?"

"Hell, girls don't do anything that ain't on purpose."

He was walking all slumped down, dragging his feet in the dust. "You want to know something? We're going to be just like that someday."

"Like what?"

"Like him. Sitting around talking about now. Looking at the kids, saying everything's different, saying how things used to be."

"What the hell you talking about?"

"Me," Billy said. "Sixty–seventy years from now it'll be me sitting, talking like that."

"You could be dead by then."

"Never happen. I'll be sitting there."

I tried to see Billy teetering on a chair, telling stories. It didn't work. "Why would you want to do that anyway?"

"Nothing to do with want to or not want to. Just the way things are."

"I thought you wanted to be on a river boat."

"Sure," Billy said. "That's what I told Great-Gramps. He just laughed. He said that didn't have nothing to do with it. He said so it'll be on some old houseboat down toward St. Louis or somewhere. Place doesn't make no difference. He said I'll end up like him, sitting in a chair, watching the young ones chase girls up and down the country roads."

We went on walking. The air was cooler close to the river, the dusty smell gone. Lightning bugs were flashing in the weeds close to the water and a screech owl was going at it someplace. Billy tossed a pebble at the edge of the water. The ripples moved out into the moonlight. The rest of the water stayed dark and the spreading circles seemed to be floating in space.

Billy had a funny, stubborn look.

"What's wrong with you?" I said.

"I already told you." He still had that look. "Come on, Steve."

"Where?"

"Up to the tavern. See if we can find a beer."

I'd never done any more than taste beer. "What do you mean, find one?"

"Sure," he said. "Somebody don't finish a bottle. Bartender still puts it back in the case. You get there right after he shoves an empty case out back and you maybe find half a bottle still cold."

I remembered some of the men I'd seen going in and out of the tavern. "Can't tell who's been sucking on those things."

"Beer's a disinfectant," Billy said.

"It is not."

"Sure. It's a mild acid with certain disinfectant properties."

I just looked at him.

"Sure. Old man Smithers said so. Down at the drugstore they were arguing about it one day."

Billy picked up a big chunk of broken blacktop and threw it, and the moonlight on the river blew into a million pieces, then began fitting back together again.

I moved around, trying to see his face. "What's the matter with you?"

"I told you."

"No you didn't."

"Don't you listen?"

"Yes."

"No you don't. You don't listen to anything."

Billy started laughing but there was a twist to his mouth I'd never seen before. "Goddamnit, Steve, I been trying to tell you. I'm going to be the oldest man in the world someday."

He walked away, up toward the back of the tavern, going fast.

I started after him. "Billy, wait a minute!"

He didn't answer. I stopped and watched him go, then headed back up the street to find my brothers at the poolhall and tell them I was ready anytime they were.

Billy's Great-Gramps was sitting in front of the station all by himself. I walked up close. He had his eyes closed. He might have been dead for all I could tell. I stared at him for a long time. He did look a little bit like Billy. Finally he moved enough to start his chair rocking back and forth, but he didn't open his eyes.

I walked on to the poolhall. I didn't know what I would have said to him anyway. It just seemed, if I could only think of the right question, that somebody who was the Oldest Man in the World would surely have something important to tell me.

4

I still saw Billy around school every day, but from that night on it seemed he was two or three years older and didn't have time to wait for me to catch up. He'd started smoking and would light up every chance he got, take a few puffs, then pinch the cigarette out and put the butt in his pocket. I kept trying to talk to him, but he always seemed to have a girl backed into a corner, leaning over her, his hand on the wall above her shoulder.

A couple of weeks later I ran into him on a Saturday night at High Ridge. I'd ridden along with Lars and Erik to a wedding dance in the old hall up above the tavern. Main Street was lined with cars. We had to pull off into the alley behind the cheese factory to park.

My brothers went into the tavern. The music wasn't playing yet up in the dance hall, so I waited outside, listening to the talk about dry weather, no corn, and oats going to be all chaff. It could have been the same men who were always talking at the filling station in Gordon's Landing.

There was a burst of music from the hall.

"Hey," someone said, "how come there's all these wedding dances again?"

A man grinned. "I hear the tavern keeper's taking credit. Says he's putting pin holes in the rubbers he sells."

I was about to go upstairs when Billy came out of the tavern. His arm was around a fat looking girl and he had on a necktie and was smoking a cigar. It was the first time I'd seen him wearing a tie.

"Hiya, Steve!" he yelled.

"Hi, Billy. What you been doing?"

He leaned up close and winked. "I been finding out what girls are for."

His face was red and I could smell the beer. He rolled the cigar back and forth in his mouth, sending up a big blue cloud. For awhile we stood there looking at each other like two old men who hadn't met since they were in first grade together.

"When we going to ride the train again?" I asked.

Billy took the cigar out of his mouth and tapped the ashes off the end. "That's kid stuff."

"Yeah, I guess so."

He gave the girl a hug and she giggled. "This is Flora. Bunch of us are going down to French Prairie. Want to come?"

"I got to stay with my brothers."

"Okay, Kid. See you around."

"Sure."

I watched Billy and the girl pile into an old Chrysler along with about six others. The starter ground over a few times and quit. The boys got out and pushed the car until it started, then piled in again. With the smoke from Billy's cigar pouring out the back window, they went roaring off toward French Prairie, a bigger place with things always going on. I felt I'd just been told to go blow my nose.

The polka music and the sound of stomping feet came down from the dance hall. I started up the stairs, then changed my mind and walked across the street to a little beer bar. Back in the dark end of the place I ordered a beer, trying to act as though I'd done that a thousand times. The man behind the bar didn't even look at me, just banged the bottle down and took my money.

It was the first time I'd done anything more than try a sip or two. I tipped the bottle up and forced the beer down until the bitterness was gone and it started tasting all right. By the time I was halfway through the bottle I could feel the glow starting. I took a deep breath and looked around. A blond boy was watching me.

"Pretty good stuff," I said.

"Yeah. Been up to the dance yet?"

"I just got here. You?"

He held up his bottle of beer. "I'm still getting ready."

I finished mine and we ordered another. I could feel my shirt getting wet and sticking to my back. The jukebox was playing and it sounded as if about five hundred people were all talking at once.

The blond boy nudged me. "Somebody said there's lots of extra girls up there tonight. You got a car?"

"I came with my brothers."

"Tough to make out if you ain't got a car." He tipped up his bottle and took a long drink. "But what the hell? You can always make out if you put your mind to it."

"Sure," I said.

"I guess you do all right."

With my fingernail I worked at tearing a little circle in the middle of the wet beer bottle label. "Well, you know how it is."

"Sure." He took another drink and looked down into the mouth of the bottle. Then he laughed. "Oh, what the hell! You want to know something? I don't know how it is at all. I'm going to be eighteen one of these days and I'm still a damn virgin. What do you think of that?"

I couldn't think of anything to say.

He laughed again. "I wouldn't be telling you this if I knew you. Wouldn't be telling you anyway wasn't for the beer. I've never even had my hand on what my brother calls 'that third ultimate' let alone get my thing within range."

I finished a third beer, my hand in slow motion when I put the empty bottle down on the bar. My shirt was wet all over and I could tell by the feel that my face was red.

"You going over to the dance?" I said.

He shook his head. "I only had three beers. I got to have four before I stop remembering I don't dance so good."

Outside, the air was moving a little and my wet shirt all at once turned cold all over. I had a feeling I should be wearing a trench coat with the collar turned up and maybe a little smile on my face the way I felt sometimes coming out of a movie. Everyone seemed to be turning to look at me and I walked very carefully across the street and climbed the steep stairs to the hall.

People were going by like couples on a merry-go-round. I leaned against the wall, trying to see through the smoke. The wall boards weren't painted and the rough lumber scratched through my shirt.

A line-up of girls sat on chairs along the side, all leaning forward a little and smiling as though they were really happy. Every now and then one would pat her hair and play button-button up and down the front of her dress to make sure she was put together right and all the time looking around to see if anybody was coming for her.

The dancers were moving by so fast they didn't have any faces, until a couple did a little whirl right in front of me. The girl's face stopped whirling long enough for her to look over the boy's shoulder and wink at me. They whirled away again and I lost her face, but I could see she was something like the one who had been with Billy. A lot prettier and not fat, but the same look of waiting for just about anything to come along and happen.

The same girl came by again. She looked at me so I held up one finger for the next dance. She nodded and kept on looking at me, snapping her head around in a whirl, then freezing her eyes on me at the end of each turn in a way that made me dizzy.

She was standing by herself after the music stopped. I walked up behind her. She had on a spicy perfume that reminded me of Christmas. I was quite a bit taller and could look over her shoulders and see her blouse sticking out in front. I thought of the blond boy. Were those ultimates one and two? I didn't say anything. Finally she laughed and turned around as though she already knew who it was.

"You winked at me," I said.

She laughed. "Sure. Because you were looking at me that way."

"What way?"

She put her hands up, fanned her hair up off her neck and let it fall. "You know what way."

The music began. My head was spinning. I felt a thousand years old and locked away with her in some dark place where we could do anything we wanted.

We started dancing, stiff at first because we were trying to look at each other. Then she took a deep breath and came up close. I took long steps, feeling her legs against me, sometimes dancing at half speed with the music and she followed, keeping perfect time.

At the end of that number, or maybe sometime later, a boy came up and asked her for a dance.

She stepped back a little and looked at me. "Do I have the next dance?"

"Sure. I wrote it down somewhere." I began going through my pockets.

The boy was grinning, kind of ducking his head down at us. One lock of hair kept falling over his forehead. Each time, he very carefully took the lock of hair between his thumb and little finger and put it exactly back into place in the deep wave he had.

"You're just going to have to take my word for it," I said.

"And she has the next and the next, I suppose?"

I touched her arm. "The next and the next?"

"I suppose," she said.

He moved away, looking back at us, smiling, the lock of hair down on his forehead again.

I turned to her. For a minute something happened in my head as though the beer had quit all at once. She was separated from all the noise and people, wearing a tight-fitting white blouse with bird decorations on it. Her skirt had a bright band around the bottom and it kept whirling a little even when she didn't seem to be moving, as though something was happening in there. I remembered a song Billy had been singing in school lately — "I'll meet you in Pettycoat Lane, just inside the outskirts." Her lipstick was bright red, matching the bird decorations. Little blue veins showed at her temples and her skin was a deep tan, reminding me of the Gypsy women who stopped at the farm sometimes, coming out of their dark, painted-up caravans, then going back inside into a world I didn't know anything about. Her blouse was lifting up and down with her breathing.

"You're looking at me that way again," she said.

I reached for her, wishing I had skipped the last beer because now it was all getting foggy and I wanted it to stay sharp and clear. I didn't even know what music was playing. I was talking and didn't remember what the words were by the time they came out of my mouth. She kept laughing and touching the back of my neck. The music stopped every now and then. Each time, we moved into a corner and stayed close, keeping time to what had been playing, then whirled out onto the floor when the music started again.

"How old are you?"

It was kind of an echo. I guess she'd been saying it for quite awhile.

"Seventeen." I blurted it out and knew I should have added a year or two.

She laughed.

"What about you?"

She looked at me. I could see the wheels going around and around in her head. "Will it make any difference to you?"

I shook my head.

"I'm eighteen." She watched my face. "It doesn't matter?"

"No." I pulled her closer and we went on dancing, hardly moving our feet. I started thinking of the Gypsy women again with their skirts swinging and their hands always reaching out.

Her fingers tightened on my neck and she gave me a little shake. The music had stopped. The hall was half empty.

"It's intermission," she said.

My feet were still trying to move back and forth. I finally got everything sorted out and we went down the stairs, clumping hard on each step, laughing, arms around each other.

The cool outside air lifted at my wet clothes. Holding tight and not talking, we went across the street and stopped in front of the beer bar. The neon light turned us both red. With my finger I traced the outline of color on her face. She turned her head and trapped my hand between her cheek and shoulder.

"Want a beer or something?"

She looked through the window at the crowd. The noise was making the glass move in and out. "Not in there."

"Maybe I could sneak a couple out."

"Okay."

The blond boy was sitting in a booth, trying to fill a glass and mostly was missing. I ordered two cans of beer and went over to him while I waited.

"I think you got ready too long."

He blinked and finally remembered me. "Might be right. Best part is, can't remember what I was getting ready for."

"Something about a third ultimate."

"Go to hell, you bastard." He gave up trying to pour the beer and sprawled back in the booth.

When I went out, she didn't see me for a minute and her face was different, looking off at something a couple million miles away. I reached out to touch her with the cold beer to make her jump, but she was somebody else now so I didn't do that. I waited, shifting my weight from one foot to the other until she saw me. Her wide smile came back, covering up whatever it was that had been on her face.

She moved close, her shoulder touching me.

"We can't drink them here," I said.

"All right."

"I guess we better take a walk or something."

She laughed. "Sure. Walk or something."

I put both cans of beer in one hand, down out of sight. She had hold of my other arm and we started taking long, zig-zagging steps, our legs hitting. I didn't even think about where we were going, but then we were turning into the alley back of the cheese factory where the car was parked.

It was a two-door sedan. When I opened the door, she swung the front seat out of the way and got into the back as if she'd been in that car a thousand times.

I got in after her and rolled all the windows down. She leaned back and fanned out her hair, the sparks flashing. I could just barely make out her face above the white blouse. The cushions creaked as she let out a long breath and settled lower. I leaned back beside her and when I turned I could feel her hair, warm under my cheek.

"Have a beer." I held it out and was cold all at once.

Her hand found the can. "Here's to us."

I took a long drink and shivered. She put her hand on my shoulder. "What's the matter?"

"Rabbit jumped over my grave."

"What's that mean?"

"I don't know. Just a saying."

"Rabbits," she said.

I took another long drink. It began to help and I tried to put my arm around her but my hand hit her beer can and tipped it. She jumped.

"Hey! That's cold."

"Sorry."

I took out my handkerchief and reached over. "Where?"

"In front." She was laughing.

I still wasn't sure. Then I remembered a story Billy's Great Grandfather had told about a man measuring a woman for a dress. He put two marks on her in front, with chalk. "What's that for?" the woman said. "Pockets," the man said. "I don't want pockets," she said and he said, "OK, no pockets" and started rubbing the chalk out.

"I can't see," I said.

She took my hand and guided me. I dabbed at her blouse. She took a deep breath and leaned back. I had to do something with the can of beer in my other hand. I finished that and put the can down.

She was moving her hands around. When I reached out, she had unbuttoned her blouse part way. A light flashed somewhere outside and I jumped. For a second I could see her leaning back, looking at me, laughing.

I was cold again. I didn't know what I was supposed to do next. A long way off, the music started in the hall. For a minute I wanted to run back to the dance, wanted the music to be the school bell ringing, saving me just as I was about to get into a fight I knew I was going to lose.

I tried to get a picture in my mind of the two of us tangled up together on the seat. I could never get past the beginning. Something happened in my head, the way it had up in the hall. I was somebody else this time, looking at the two of us on the car seat. I was glad it wasn't someplace where Billy, or the blond boy or the Oldest Man in the World could see I had a third ultimate right in front of me and didn't know what to do with it. She was still laughing and she took my hand and showed me.

The music had been playing and stopping and playing again. She wasn't laughing anymore. I ran my fingers over her face and she wasn't smiling either.

The music stopped and didn't start up again. Back on the main street, somebody was calling a name. Jenny maybe, or Gemmy. She pulled away from me and put herself together, moving very quickly. "I got to go. You stay here."

"No."

She leaned over and kissed me. "Here's to our luck."

She started to get out. I held her and wouldn't let her go.

"I'll be here next Saturday night," she said.

I tried to get out, but she held me back and slipped away. I could see her running toward the street, fast and straight, not flopping her feet around the way some girls did. At the end of the alley she slowed down and walked around the corner.

"Here she is," a boy's voice called.

A car door slammed. Tires squealed. I could hear the car move away, and I leaned back, trying to remember the evening from the beginning. I thought about Billy and the fat girl named Flora and wondered how he'd made out. "To hell with Billy," I said.

I was half asleep when my brothers came. The car started off, neither of them talking, and we were home before I woke up enough to realize I didn't even know her name or where she lived.

After Lars and Erik went inside, I stood in the yard looking around. A light wind was moving in the tops of the pines and maple trees. The stars were flickering the way they do on a hot night in mid-summer. They shouldn't have been doing that in May. I could see a little mist hanging in the ravine leading down toward the river. An owl was hooting, to the west where the woods was a black shape against the sky. The house stayed dark. I looked at it sitting there, and I could have been six or seven years old, sneaking out through a window in the middle of the night to see what was happening while everyone was asleep. I didn't understand how it could all be just the same as ever.

Before I went in, I remembered to get the two beer cans out of the car and hide them.

At school on Monday, I started working on Billy, when I could get him away from the girls, to go to High Ridge next Saturday. "Naw," he said. "Never go to the same place twice in a row. Why you want to go there so bad?"

"I met this girl at the dance."

"Who is she?"

I hesitated. "Well, that's a funny thing. I got so busy I forgot to ask."

Billy laughed and whacked me on the shoulder. "There, you see. You're going to be the oldest man in the world someday, too."

"What'd you guys do in French Prairie?"

"Got drunk. Got laid."

On Saturday night I rode part way with my brothers, then hitched to High Ridge. For a long time I went around and around the edge of the dance floor, trying to get a close look at all the girls, but she wasn't there.

Over at the beer bar, the blond boy had three empty bottles on the table already.

"How you making out?" I asked.

He blinked at me, remembering. "Goddamnit, I already told you! I ain't making out!"

All at once I felt about ten years older. "Well, don't give up. Lots of girls over there."

"Great. One more beer and I'll go get me one."

There was another wedding dance in High Ridge the next Saturday night. Lars was heading that way and he let me ride along.

I walked around and around the dance floor again, but I couldn't find her. The blond boy was in the bar and he wasn't going to make it to the dance this time either. I drank a beer, wondering if I should tell him that finding the third ultimate didn't automatically solve everything, but he seemed happy the way he was.

I made several more trips back and forth across the street, then met Lars coming down the stairs. "Hey," he said. "I was looking for you. You want to stay here?"

"No!"

He looked at me closely. "Couldn't find anybody interesting?"

I hadn't told him about the girl. We never talked to each other about that kind of thing. "Not the one I was looking for."

"Girl?"

I nodded.

He was one step above me on the stairs and seemed about twenty years older. Then, maybe because he'd been drinking a little, he put his arm around my shoulders. He'd never done that before. "What the hell?" he said, "you'll find somebody else."

We walked down the stairs. "I was thinking of leaving. Going down to Gordon's Landing to line up a ballgame for tomorrow. All right?"

"Sure."

We didn't talk in the car. I had never seen him with a girl. The gang he ran around with was always playing ball and cards and drinking a lot of beer. The idea of Lars knowing what it was like to lose somebody was a new idea. I wanted to talk more with him and didn't know how. I wanted to ask how come you don't go out with girls? When you get the car almost anytime you want, how come you hang around here instead of going off to bigger, more exciting places?

In Gordon's Landing Lars went over to the tavern and I headed for the filling station. A few of the usual hang-around bunch were there and the Oldest Man in the World was teetering back in his chair. I leaned against one of the gaspumps still thinking about the girl at High Ridge.

"I can tell you one thing," the old man was saying, "in my day we didn't waste time going around complaining the sky was falling all the time."

He started laughing. "Say, you know those humps in the road down along the river? You know why those things are called 'thank-you-ma'ams?'

Well, Sir, you'd get yourself a girl in the buggy and start down that road. When everything was just right, you'd get the horse to going good and hit one of those humps. All you had left to do was say 'thank-you-ma-am!' "

The men teetered and laughed, but they seemed half asleep. Pretty soon they all left. I was still standing by the gaspump, not even sure the old man had seen me until he said, "Sit down, Boy. Too late to be standing up like that."

I took the chair next to his and teetered back.

"By God I'm sure glad everybody went home. I never heard so much talk in all my life about no rain, no corn and everybody arguing over what year the grasshoppers ate everything."

"It is dry," I said.

"Sure. Dry other years. Be dry again. Rain again, too. Little dry weather don't mean the world's coming to the end. Seems like everybody's just busting a gut seein' who can invent the biggest disaster, proud as hell his cornfield's dryer than the next man's. Hell's bells, if I'd give up everytime anything went wrong, I'd been dead eighty years ago."

I thought of Dad looking at the clouds and letting the dry soil run through his hands, and I felt myself getting stubborn. "Well, on a farm, you don't get rain, you got a lot to worry about."

"Hell, there's things more important than losing crops. That's all I'm saying. Been saying it all night. And it ain't forever like some things are."

I teetered back and forth, feeling as old as he was. "Yeah. Losing people is worse."

He didn't say anything for a minute, just leaned forward trying to look at my face. I could hear voices over at the tavern. A car went by with the radio playing. What the hell am I doing, I thought. It's Saturday night and I'm sitting around talking with the Oldest Man in the World, saying things I wouldn't even say to Billy.

"Well," he said. "Well. I guess maybe you found yourself that first one."

I nodded.

"What happened?"

"I lost her again already."

"The hell you did? You look for her?"

"Sure."

He teetered back. "Anything else you can do to find her?"

"I don't think so." Could I keep going back to High Ridge every Saturday night? Could I tap people on the shoulder and say, "Did you see me with a girl here that time? Do you know who she is?" Could I check all the cars in the alley for one that was rocking back and forth a little?

"I don't think there's anything else I can do."

"Well, then I guess you got to find yourself another one."

"Just forget her?"

"Nope. Find another one. 'Cause losing one's just as likely as finding one. Always has been."

I thought about Eva Mae who was probably sleeping somewhere behind the wall where we sat. The day with her seemed a long time back.

The old man stretched and looked out over the river. "Wouldn't you think those fool lightning bugs would get tired flashing on and off?"

"Hey," I said. "Did you really see that buffalo?"

"Buffalo?"

"You know. Out on Elm Tree Island. With the wolves."

"I saw it. At least I think I did. You got to remember it gets hard to keep things straight. Like someday you're going to get that girl you can't find all mixed up with some other girl. But I saw that buffalo all right."

He told the whole story all over again, but longer this time. I could see the blood on the white and hear the cold snow crunching under his feet. When he stopped talking I was surprised to find it wasn't the middle of winter.

"Hell," he said. "I don't suppose there's even a wolf left around now, let alone a buffalo."

"I know where there're some wolves," I said. "I mean, I did. There's this wild valley close to our farm. Used to be a den of wolves down there and we'd hear them howl. Haven't heard them now for three, four years."

"Well, if you find one, don't tell anybody. Don't even tell me.

Cause I might forget and say something. And those same bastards that're so proud they got the driest fields wouldn't have a day of peace until they killed the last wolf this side of Canada."

"Why would they want to do that?"

"Bounty. Leastwise that's what they'd tell you. I figure they just can't stand the idea of something running loose. Hell, I wasn't that much better myself."

"You still go hunting?"

He shook his head.

"Why'd you quit?"

"Don't know. Either got too smart or got too old. You hunt, Boy?"

"Sure."

"You remember what it feels like, having a running deer locked in out in front of your sights?"

I thought about looking along the cold blue of the .22 rifle barrel and the red fox color of a squirrel running but the gun moving, too, so the squirrel seemed to be stopped. "Not a deer. I remember with a squirrel."

"Same thing. Idea is to stop 'em running. What about that girl? When you was getting your shot at her, wasn't it the same way?"

I didn't like the way his question made me feel. That wasn't how I thought about her. At least not the only way. I tried to think of something safe to say that wouldn't get twisted around to the same subject. By the time I decided to ask about passenger pigeons, he was fast asleep.

I went across the street and got into the car. The voices were louder than ever in the tavern. My head was full of buffalo, squirrels, deer and girls all scrambled up together, running away from me. I wondered if I'd know her if she came walking up the street. In the car I'd know her, all right.

5

The next Monday was only the first week of June, but because school was out and the weather so hot and dry, it seemed like the middle of summer.

I was still the one who went for the horses every morning. Just before we finished milking, Dad caught my eye and gave a nod. I went running down the lane, following the twists and turns of the narrow paths, making racing car noises and feeling ten years old again.

The horses were in the farthest corner of the woods, all crowded together, standing still, trying to hide. I sneaked around them, then jumped up, waving my arms and yelling. They reared around and galloped off, hoofs pounding, reminding me of a western movie with the cavalry coming or the Indians riding in a circle around the wagons.

The bay mare we called Tess stopped to pull at some grass. I ran up, grabbed her mane, swung onto her back and sent her galloping after the others.

I stayed on when she jumped the ditch, but a low limb knocked me back across her rump and I went rolling into the hazel brush and blackberry vines, hearing the hoofbeats leaving me behind.

By the time I caught up, they had stopped to graze by the gnarled willow where the grass was greener. I sat down and let them alone. Out of sight, down the little ravine, was the log cabin Erik and I had built several years before. I had spent about half of my life in that woods. Now I sat on the hillside and that other boy was still down there, maybe starting a fire in the cabin stove, and I was somebody else now.

I got to the house just in time for breakfast. Mom looked at my legs. "You're not wet," she said.

I hadn't even noticed. Other years I would have been wet halfway to the crotch from the dew on the grass and wildflowers.

"I had the radio on," Mom said. "Everybody's talking about how dry it is." She looked at Erik. "The radio quit."

I thought of the old man. "Been dry other years."

"That doesn't help us get a crop this time," Dad said.

Erik was frowning at his plate. "Did it make a screeching noise again?"

"It just quit," Mom said.

Dad finished his coffee. "Well, this isn't getting any hay put up." He stopped for a minute in the kitchen and talked with Mom. She was looking up at him and his hand was on her shoulder. It didn't have anything to do with chasing girls up the wainscoting or locking them into your sights to stop them running. It was the first time I'd thought about them being young once and maybe wondering what everything was all about.

Erik began working on the radio.

Lars and I had the horses all harnessed when Dad stuck his head around the horsebarn door. There was the white of ground feed on his overalls from feeding the pigs. "Where's Erik?"

"Haven't seen him since breakfast."

"Well, see if you can find him."

I found Erik still fiddling with the radio, getting some funny squeaks out of it. "Hey," I said, "we're supposed to be working."

He blinked at me, a lock of hair over his forehead, reminding me of the tall boy at High Ridge. He looked at the empty table. "Oh, I didn't know you'd gone out."

We started the haying. Sometimes it seemed that every summer I could remember had been just one long, unending day in the hayfields. As soon as one field was finished, we'd start another. By the time the last field was put up, the first one was starting to bloom, ready to be cut again.

Except for the dryness and heat, this summer should have been just like any other year. But it wasn't. My mind kept wandering off beyond the horizon—the girl at High Ridge, the stories at the filling station, Billy acting differently now, the Oldest Man in the World talking about chasing girls, trying to remember their names.

I led the horse on the hayrope each time we came in with a load. Once I just about pulled the hayfork right out through the end of the barn and then stood there thinking about being in the back seat of the car.

On Wednesday night I woke and heard the storm begin, first the wind in the trees, the flash of lightning, too far off to make thunder, then a rattle of rain on the window. I waited until it settled into a steady shower, pulled the covers up and went back to sleep, knowing tomorrow would be different.

The sun was higher than usual when I woke and I wondered if I had gone back to sleep after being called. Then I heard Dad's voice.

"By God, wait a month for rain and the minute you get some good hay down, damned if it doesn't rain just enough to get it wet."

"If it waited to be the right time, it never would rain," Mom said.

Dad didn't send me to get the horses and at breakfast we could see him thinking about the day. He liked to go fishing at the Mississippi, but there was the problem of thistles that needed cutting. Finally he smiled at us and said "In the great scheme of things, I guess it's not going to matter if we let the thistles go a day or two longer."

He was thinking about it and frowning, though. "Still, in one day, more will go to seed."

Mom laughed. "Still, if you never take a day off, you might go to seed, too."

He patted her hand. "Thank you."

He got up. "Well, talking's not going to get any fishworms dug."

"All dug," Lars said.

"Just how did you know we were going fishing?"

Lars grinned. "Well the odds were pretty good. I saw you twist the hay and shake your head. But mostly you didn't get the thistle-cutting tools out before breakfast."

Dad laughed. Mom fixed us a lunch, saying she might go and see if the black raspberries were ripe. She liked to get out into the woods all by herself and seemed to need the berries for an excuse, just the way Dad needed the rain before he could go fishing.

With the cane fishpoles tied over the car in a long arc, we headed for the river. The air was still cool from the rain, the sky so clear that each ridge stood out like a separate world, but when we started down the steep hill to Gordon's Landing, everything began to change. There were walnut trees along the road. The air was warm and steamy when we got to the bottom of the hill.

Dad told Lars to pull in at the station for gas. The old man was out front at the pumps. "Hello, Boy," he said. "Don't see you much by daylight."

"Hello, Bill." I'd never called him by name before. It seemed as though I should be saying "mister" when I spoke to the Oldest Man in the World. Dad was looking at me, frowning.

I moved away, afraid the old man would say something that might get me in trouble. People up on the ridges were suspicious of places like Gordon's Landing. When anything bad happened anywhere along the Mississippi, somebody was sure to nod a certain way and I always knew what was coming: "Well, you know what they say; 'the Devil spends extra time in a river town.' "

Dad and the old man just talked about fishing, then we drove up the river to a place called Elm Springs. The spring bubbled up out of the sand right beside the road and ran in a little stream down to the slough. We got our gear into a rowboat, moving in slow motion because we had all the time in the world.

Dad rowed, sending us across the slough in long, easy sweeps, and we tied the boat to a willow near the railroad bridge. The sun was bright, the air very still. Hawks wheeled slowly against the blue sky along the high bluffs. Up-river I could see Lover's Leap and I thought of Eva Mae up there with the wind pushing her dress against her. Suddenly I remembered and checked the poles along the tracks. The blue insulators had all been replaced. With Dad sitting there in the boat with me, I couldn't believe Billy and I had done that.

When the sun was almost straight above us, we pulled the boat under the shade of the bridge and ate our lunch there on the rocks. For quite awhile the squeak of oarlocks came from out on the river, and finally a big, flat-bottomed rowboat with a funny-looking winch at the stern came under the bridge. The man rowing was maybe Dad's age, with a fuzz of black whiskers and dark-rimmed eyes.

"Hey," Dad called, "we've got one of your boats."

The man let the big boat drift up close to the rocks. "You gonna be all day?"

"Sure."

"Make it seventy five cents then."

Dad gave him the money and he rowed on across the slough toward the landing at Elm Springs.

"What's he do with that funny boat?" I asked.

"He's a clammer," Dad said. "Gets clams off the bottom of the river for the shells."

"What for?"

"Buttons. Mother of pearl buttons they call them when they've got the shiny part on them."

"Why mother of pearl?"

"I don't know. Never thought about that."

"Because the pearl, when there is one, is on the inside and gets made by the clam which is on the outside and that makes it kind of the pearl's mother," Erik said, looking as usual as though he'd been waiting about ten years for somebody to ask the question.

"We don't call a cow 'mother of calf'."

"But you could," Erik said.

"I never saw him before," I said.

Dad laughed. "Well, he's an off-again, on-again clammer."

I looked at Erik. "That means he drinks," Erik explained.

Lars hadn't said anything for a long time. I looked around and he was leaning back against the rocks, asleep, a half-eaten sandwich in his hand and a batch of yellowjackets working away at the meat filling.

We caught a few blue gills during the afternoon, then rowed back to the landing, moving in that same slow motion. I was already in the back seat of the car when I saw the girl standing on the path about halfway between the spring and the tarpaper-covered shack at the edge of the woods. There was a water bucket in her hand, the outside covered with condensation so I knew she had already been to the spring. She was staring up into the trees and I suddenly realized the whole place was filled with moving colors, dozens of redstarts hanging like Christmas tree ornaments on the branches of the willows. She didn't seem to know we were there.

I couldn't stop looking at her. She was barefoot and wearing a faded dusty-blue dress. It was sleeveless and her arms were slim and tanned. Her hair was brown, with streaks from the sun. She was small and fine-featured and maybe should have looked out of place there with her bucket of water. She didn't look out of place. She was the prettiest girl I had ever seen.

Erik started the engine and pulled out onto the road. The redstarts swarmed up with a rattle of wings. The whole woods was moving. The girl saw us and her eyes seemed to flash bright blue. I had the car window down. I wanted to reach out to her. I wanted to yell, "Stop the car!"

She turned, looking after us. I started laughing, thinking how it would be to ask if we could stop instead of hurrying home to milk the cows, because of how some barefoot girl I had never seen before happened to look as she stood on a dusty path in front of a tarpaper shack.

Lars was in back with me. "What's the matter with you?"

"Nothing."

He looked at me suspiciously but he hadn't seen her.

On Sunday afternoon Lars and Erik went down to Gordon's Landing for a baseball game and I rode along. Right after we got there a long argument started over a play at second base. The umpire took off his glasses to read the rule book. When they got the argument settled, he couldn't find his glasses. While everyone looked, the two pitchers went to get a case of beer.

Billy was playing left field. I walked out and asked him if he knew the girl.

"Sure," he said.

"Well for crying out loud! How come you never said anything about her?"

He shrugged. "I don't know." He kicked the ground, cleaning out the cleats of his baseball shoes.

"Well for crying out loud! She's the prettiest girl I ever saw."

Billy looked up and grinned. "Is she? I never paid any mind. Maybe because she's my cousin."

I stared at him.

"Sure she is. Her old man's my drinking uncle." Billy gave a big wink and moved up close and whispered, "And at our house we don't even talk about what became of her mother."

I guess I was staring at him again because he laughed.

"Want to go see her?"

"Well, sure."

He took off his glove. "Come on."

"You mean right now?"

"Sure." He tossed the glove down and walked off the field.

"Hey!" the center fielder yelled.

Billy waved at him and kept walking. "Nobody's ever going to hit a ball in this game anyway."

He had the pickup truck from the filling station. We got in and drove off, leaving the center fielder standing in the dust behind us, still yelling.

As we headed up along the bottom of the bluffs for Elm Springs, Billy started singing. "The prettiest girl I ever saw was sipping cider through a straw." He stopped the truck in front of the shack. "There she is." He pointed across the road to the shore of the slough.

She was sitting on an overturned rowboat, reading a book, wearing bluejeans this time and looking smaller and younger.

"Hi, Anne," Billy said.

She put the book down behind her. "Hi, Billy." She looked at me for a second. Something in her face seemed to change and I wondered if she remembered. But mostly I just stared at her, not thinking anything.

"His name's Steve," Billy said. "He's all right."

She looked at me again for a long moment.

Billy laughed. "Sometimes he talks. A little while ago he said you were the prettiest girl he ever saw."

I felt my face getting red. Her eyes were blue all right. The whites had blue in them, too. After what seemed like a month a little smile started at one corner of her mouth and slowly got bigger.

"Billy's an awful liar."

"Not all the time."

She laughed, hugged her knees and teetered back a little on the boat. There didn't seem to be anything she could do that didn't make her prettier.

Billy looked across the slough to where the big rowboat with the winch was crawling along way out in the main part of the river. "The Old Man at it?"

She nodded.

"I guess he didn't find any pearls lately."

"Not lately."

"Shells are money, too," Billy said. He dipped a rusty can in the spring and watched me while he drank.

I pointed to the book laying cover-down on the rowboat. "What're you reading?"

She looked at it quickly, then back at me. *"Alice in Wonderland."* She was very still while she waited for me to say something.

"I never read it, but my mother likes it."

She smiled. Billy cleared his throat. "Ah, sooner or later I really should get back to left field."

Anne laughed. "You're crazy."

"Sure," Billy said. "Want to come to the ballgame?"

She shook her head and looked out toward the big rowboat on the river.

"There's an excursion steamboat coming," I finally managed to say. "To French Prairie. Next Friday night." Her blue eyes were on me. "You — want to go?"

She stood up for the first time, her face so serious I was sure she was going to say no. She came a step closer, not quite as tall as I had thought, her eyes just about even with my shoulders.

"Is it real fancy? I mean, a plain white dress, would that be all right?"

"Sure."

Her face lighted up with that slow smile again. "I'd like to go."

"About 7:30," I said, wanting to say something more or maybe reach out and touch her.

Billy cleared his throat again. "Left field?"

We drove back to the game. It was just starting again. Billy walked out onto the field, put on his glove and caught a long fly ball as though it had all been planned that way.

6

The steamboat was a fancy paddlewheeler that came up the Mississippi from New Orleans each summer. It had a big dance floor and band and it stopped at a different river port each night for a "moonlight excursion." People called it that even if it was raining. I had seen the boat from shore, but I'd never been on it before.

On the way home from the ballgame I began working on Lars and Erik to go so I'd be sure to have a ride. They said they were going to a card game that night.

"Anyway," Lars said, "those things are pretty dumb. Bunch of people crowding around, looking at the shore they just came from, saying ooh and aah like they never saw it before. That's no fun unless. . . ."

He suddenly looked at me. "You taking a girl?"

"Yes."

"Well, well. Little brother's growing up."

"Who is she?" Erik asked.

"I'm not going to tell you."

"We'll find out if we go."

"But probably you're not going, so you won't find out."

Erik grinned. "Maybe we better go just to have a look at her."

In the end they decided on the card game, but at least they didn't say anything about it at home.

For the next couple of days I kept trying to think of some way to get a ride, even making a few phone calls when no one was around to hear. I didn't talk to Mom and Dad about it because that would have left me sitting out there in plain sight with their eyes trained on me like telescopes, especially when it was a girl from along the river who lived in a tarpaper shack.

There was one possibility I kept putting off, these three brothers who lived down in the valley from us. They had a sixteen-cylinder Packard that was about eight feet tall, had jump-seats in the back and pull-down shades on the windows. The story was that it came from a Chicago bootlegger who had a still in their barn one summer.

I'd gone fishing with the brothers sometimes. They seemed all right to me, but not many people liked them. All you had to do was mention their last name and someone would say something like "over the hill to the poor house is where that bunch is headed." My parents didn't think much of them either, but mostly that was because they needed haircuts all the time.

The youngest brother was my age. He had already dropped out of school and didn't care about anything except the car. The middle one was about three years older. He was always reading books none of us had ever heard of and he drank all the time. The oldest didn't care about anything except making out. We called them Tools, Bottles and Girls. The three of them went out together a lot, Tools always driving. Every time they stopped, Tools would start working on the car. The others would come out of a tavern and find parts all over the ground, Tool's legs sticking out from underneath. Then Bottles would have another drink and Girls would start hunting again.

They weren't ideal companions for a first date, but I didn't know anything else to do, so right after chores on Wednesday I walked down to see them. The season was heading toward the longest day of the year only a couple weeks ahead and the sun was still shining. As I came down off the first hillside, a pheasant hen came out of the hazel brush and ran ahead of me. I chased her, going faster and faster and she kept leading me on, or maybe leading me away from her nest. I made a flying leap. She squawked, flew up and circled around behind me, leaving me flat on the ground, sweaty and breathing hard, still wanting to catch her even if I didn't know what I would have done except let her go again.

I went on down to the big flat rock that overlooked the main valley. The sun was still warm on my back, the meadow below in shadow. I had spent a lot of time on that rock. It was easy now to remember how I had pretended to be a lone rifleman up there, commanding the valley. I squinted and could make it happen — the group of riders, closely bunched, their horses snorting from the dust and dancing a little at being close-reined. They kept coming and I could hear voices from that earlier time.

"You men are looking into the muzzle of a Winchester '73."

They pulled up, horses' heads raised, nostrils flaring.

"There's just one of you," a man called.

"That's enough."

They were talking it over. One of them said, "Man, don't you know who that is up there?"

They turned their horses carefully and rode down the valley. "Another time," one of them yelled.

"I'll be here!"

All at once I felt silly, but I could still almost smell the dust and the sweat of those horses coming up from the empty meadow.

The rock had been other things to me, too. A place to come when I was angry, when things had gone wrong. A place to come all those times when I had to say goodbye to something or somebody I wasn't ready to lose.

The sun was going over the hilltop and I ran down into the valley to find the brothers. Everything about their farm, in its little hollow off the main valley, seemed to be in miniature. The fields were narrow strips along the dry ditch, the barn about the size of our house, their house about the size of our chicken coop. The yard was always cluttered with rusting farm machinery and old cars.

There was a sudden burst of gunfire and a lot of yelling when I got closer to the buildings. I dropped and crawled to where I could see. It was their "bouncing targets" game. They had put circles of cardboard inside old tires and carried them to the top of a hillside pasture. I could see Tools up there, rolling the tires down one at a time, some of them bouncing ten feet in the air as they hit bumps, and the others were blazing away with their .22 rifles.

I waited until the shooting stopped, then walked up the hollow, feeling as if I should be carrying a white flag. Tools was yelling something from the hillside, but I couldn't see him. Bottles, Girls and their father were sitting on the porch steps drinking beer when I joined them. There were empty rifle shells all over the ground and the smell of gunsmoke. Tools came running up in a few minutes. His clothes were all torn up and his face scratched because after the shooting stopped he had tried riding down the hill curled up inside a tractor tire. "Lasted until the first bump," he said.

The father was a small, bald man wearing bib overalls that had patches on the patches. I could see inside the house. It was a mess and I suddenly realized I had never even wondered about their mother, maybe because there was nothing about the place that had to do with a woman.

They gave me a beer and I asked if they'd like to go to the steamboat. Tools began organizing the trip, figuring out how much money they would need. They turned out their pockets, separating coins and a few bills from the .22 shells and found enough for tickets. The father dug into his pockets, too. For a minute I was worried he might be expecting to go along. He tossed a half dollar to Tools. "That'll get you a couple gallons of gas."

"I'll buy some, too," I said.

Tools took charge of the money and went to tune up the Packard.

Cattle were bawling at the door of the barn. "'Bout time to get the damned cows milked, Boys," the father said. It was almost dark by now and I wondered what Dad would think about the way they farmed.

"I'll get supper," Bottles said. He went inside and lighted a lamp. I could see him working at the stove with a book in his hand.

"That a cookbook?" I called.

He smiled. "Yeah. All about how to cook white whale meat. It's called *Moby Dick.*"

"Mopey Dick?" Girls said. He ran his hand down inside his overalls, stuck one finger out through the fly and let it dangle down. "Like this, you mean?" Girls and his father sat down on the steps laughing and clapping each other on the back until tears were running down their faces. It was so different from anything I could imagine doing with my own father that I backed away and left, feeling I had just peeked through a keyhole and wasn't ready for what I was seeing.

I made Tools shut off the cutout long before we got to Elm Springs the night of the steamboat, but it was still light and the car was in plain sight when we parked. Tools right away started trying to figure out which one of the sixteen sparkplugs was misfiring.

I went up the dusty path to the shack and knocked, my hand not making much noise on the tarpaper. The door swung open. Anne stood in the orange light from the kerosene lamp wearing a white dress. Her eyes were bright and she was smiling. Then she looked past me and her face changed. I turned and it couldn't have been much worse. Bottles was leaning against the radiator tipping up a bottle, a book in his other hand. Tools was working under the hood with his shirt off. Girls was looking out a rear window and running the shade up and down.

Anne's smile went away.

"I couldn't get a car," I said. "It was the only way I could get here."

She went on looking at the car.

I tried to think of something else to say. There was a clank of a wrench from the car. I could smell perfume very faintly. Her skin was dark and warm looking against the white of the dress. Shadflies were flapping past us, going inside to get at the kerosene lamp. Over on the Iowa side of the river a train was rumbling.

"Anne?"

She still wouldn't look at me. "I guess I don't feel like going," she said.

I could hardly hear her. She just stood there, looking past me. I reached out to take her shoulder and turn her toward me. The minute I touched the bare skin of her shoulder, she whirled and jerked away. Her head came up and she rubbed her hand across her eyes.

"Just because I live in a place like this and my father's. . . ." She started crying. I didn't dare touch her. I didn't know what to do. I was ten miles from home and had no way to get there if I told them to take their damn hearse and shove off.

"Anne, it'll be all right."

She shook her head.

There was another silence.

"You better go," she said.

"Anne, what about next week? I think I can get a car."

She turned around slowly and looked at me. There were tears on her cheeks. For a minute I thought it was going to be all right. Then she started crying again. She whirled and ran inside, the white dress floating out around her. I took a step after her. The door slammed so hard that a piece of tarpaper came loose. It started swooping from side to side, taking about three years to get down to the ground.

I waited. There wasn't a sound from inside. "Anne," I called. She didn't answer. The whippoorwills were beginning, back along the bluffs. There was a smell of dampness on the dust now. After awhile I went down the path to the car and we shoved off, south along the river road.

"What happened?" Bottles asked.

"She didn't like our looks. I think she especially didn't like the looks of you tipping up a bottle and Girls running the Goddamn shade up and down."

Girls laughed. "If they spook that easy, you're not going to make out anyway."

Bottles nodded. "That's a smart girl. I certainly wouldn't have anything to do with a bunch like us."

I was riding up front. The cutout was closed and the big car was very quiet. Tools had a big eight-day alarm clock mounted in the dash. "Ever see that magazine ad? Says at fifty miles an hour, loudest sound in a Packard is the ticking of a clock. Hear it?"

We were doing sixty, but I could hear the clock all right. I didn't want to talk anymore. I reached over and pulled the cutout cable and leaned back against the deep upholstery, listening to those sixteen cylinders blasting us toward French Prairie.

A big crowd was gathered to see the steamboat. People scattered as we roared straight at them in the big Packard. At the last second Tools swung away into a narrow parking space and stopped with the car rocking on its springs. With the exhaust roar gone we could hear the calliope playing, the off-key march music squirting out with the steam.

There was a lot of yelling and laughing near the edge of the dock. When we got up close, we saw that someone had just been pulled out of the river and stood mopping at the water with a big pink handkerchief. A bunch of men crowded in, pushing and laughing. The person had on a girl's blouse, man's pants and shoes and was wearing a lot of makeup. Water was still dripping from the curled hair at the back of the head.

"Now that he's wet he looks more like a man," someone yelled.

We pushed through toward the gangplank. The wet man stepped in front of us and batted his eyes. "One of you want to take me along?"

Everyone laughed again. Bottles moved past and we went on toward the boat.

"Why's he dressed like that?" Tools asked.

"He's a hermaphrodite," Bottles said.

"What the hell's that?" Girls said.

Bottles laughed. "You know."

"No I don't."

"It's somebody who can be a man or girl, either one."

Girls stopped and looked back, his mouth hanging open.

Bottles pushed Girls out of the way. We walked up the gangplank onto the lower deck and crowded up the stairs. On the top deck we went to the rail and looked down. The oddly-dressed person was in the middle of a tight circle of men. Three of them picked him up and threw him into the river. The crowd cheered. All I could think of was Anne. I could see her on the dusty path, leaning back, looking up at the birds, her breasts showing against the blue shirt.

Girls stared at the man in the water and his face got all twisted up the way it did when he was trying to think about something serious. "Look," he said to Bottles, "it don't figure. Why does somebody like that need us?"

Bottles smiled. "I hadn't thought of that. Maybe it doesn't work. Maybe he just makes it up."

"Makes what up?"

"One of the halves of himself," Bottles said. He was still smiling.

Girls scowled. "You're getting complicated again. You always try to make things complicated."

"No I don't."

"Yes you do! You always try to make us feel stupid!"

Bottles shook his head. "No I don't. I just like to know things. I don't do it for any other reason."

Girls face was white. "Yes you do. You do it all the time. You even do it at home, to Papa."

Girls walked away from us.

"What's going on?" I asked Bottles.

He was looking after Girls. "I don't know. I never knew he felt like that."

"Well, how come you do know so much?" Tools asked.

Bottles grinned. "Everybody needs a place to hide." He reached out and mussed up Tools' hair, seeming about eighty-nine years older than Tools and I put together.

Tools pretended to sock him in the stomach. "You're getting complicated again," he said, but he was grinning.

Bottles pointed. "He isn't."

Girls was going along the rail looking for a girl. He crowded in next to one without ever seeing her face and began rubbing up against her. She moved away from him so he backed out and went on to the next girl. She did the same thing. We followed and watched while he did that all along the rail. Finally he found one who didn't move away. She was a big girl in a yellow dress with bright red roses on it. She looked Girls over, then smiled at him.

Bottles laughed. "Why does somebody like that need us?" He put his hand on my shoulder. "You got to admit, Steve, we're a very specialized family. Only time Papa works is when the fish aren't biting. The more work there is to do, the farther away he goes to fish. Someday he'll go so far he'll never make it back. Me, I drink too much and someday I'll get so far inside a book I may not make it back either. Now Girls, he's the best shot in the family, with or without a rifle."

"What about Tools?"

"Tools?" Bottles grinned and touched Tools on the head in a benediction. "He keeps the car going. He delivers each of us to our folly."

Bottles went down the stairs toward the lower deck because he said the stokers sometimes sold bottles of whisky they kept hidden in the coal.

I stayed with Tools on the top deck. The calliope stopped. The whistle blasted and everybody cheered. Then the paddle wheel churned up the brown water. The shore began moving away from us. The way people on the dock yelled goodbye it seemed as if we were never coming back. The wet man stood all by himself, waving.

Without a girl to go with it the boat wasn't anything very special. Tools and I wandered along the decks. Quite a few girls were by themselves, but everytime I looked at one I thought of Anne in her white dress and the lamplight orange on her skin.

Tools wanted to see the engine room. We stayed there quite awhile watching the long, steam-driven connecting rods rising and falling almost in slow motion as they pushed and pulled at the big paddlewheel. Pretty soon Tools had his shirt off and was helping squirt oil on things, looking as if somebody had just given him a million dollars. I left him there and found a place all by myself way up at the bow on the lower deck, just a couple feet above the water. Over the sound of the dance music I could hear the dark river slipping by. The wind played with my hair and kept swinging my necktie up over my shoulder. From shore, the lights of houses and cars reflected out across the water.

On our way home we went up the river road. Girls wasn't with us. He had gotten off with the girl in the yellow dress when the boat dropped passengers on the Iowa side of the river.

"He'll be back in a day or two," Bottles said.

Tools double-clutched down into second and pulled the cutout open when we went by the shack at Elm Springs. The echoes bounced back from clear up at the top of the bluffs. It sounded like war had come.

"That'll fix her," Tools said.

7

I got a ride to Gordon's Landing a week later, on Sunday, and walked the two miles from there to Elm Springs. Anne was in front of the shack hanging out clothes.

"Hi," I said.

She went right on hanging up clothes.

"Aw, Anne, don't be mad."

"I'm not mad," she said, but her face didn't change and she still didn't look at me.

"Then how about some time this week?"

She turned her back and started putting in the last of her clothespins. As she stretched up to reach the line, her blouse pulled up. I could see a little bare skin at her waist. I wanted to reach out and turn her around and pull her against me. I wanted to do it fast and rough. And I wanted to do it the way I might pick up a lost puppy and cuddle it for a minute. I didn't do either, just watched her, knowing exactly where my hands would touch her.

She put in the last pin and turned.

"How about some time this week?" I repeated.

"It's too late."

"What do you mean, too late?"

"We only get one chance at anything."

For a minute I thought she was starting to cry. I didn't know what was going on. I watched her, remembering how the little smile had started on her still face that first time and then spread across like a light being turned on inside. The smile didn't come. She picked up the clothes basket and went toward the shack. She didn't even look back. When I followed, she ran inside and closed the door.

I went to the door and knocked. "Anne?"

It was the way it had been the night of the boat, as though there wasn't anybody there. Finally I went down the path and started walking back to Gordon's Landing, letting my heels bang down hard on the blacktop road, hoping she would hear and realize I had walked all that way to see her.

When I got to the filling station, a bunch of men were sitting around in the afternoon sun that was coming straight across the river. They all looked half asleep, but the same old talk was going on.

". . . and she called him a snake and he said 'that's right, but you don't have to worry.'

" 'How come?' she said. And he said 'Cause I'm just a lowly garter snake and can't ever seem to get above my name.' "

The others groaned.

Old Bill banged his pipe on his chair and got their attention. "Don't think I ever told you about two men came to me one fall, said they was headed up north to go trapping. George and Willy was their names. Going to spend the whole winter way out in the middle of nowhere. Got to worrying about going cabin crazy. I told 'em to each get a board about five feet long, cut it out in the shape of a woman and put a hole in the right place. They did that, went off north with all their trapping gear, each one carrying his board.

"Come spring, George showed up one day by himself with a batch of furs and still carrying his board. 'Where's Willy?' I said.

" 'Had to kill him,' George said.

"I asked him what happened.

" 'Well, everything was going along fine. Then one day I came in early from the trap line, found Willy fooling around with my board.' "

The young game warden was there. He was the only one who didn't laugh. "Is that kind of thing all you ever talk about?"

"Hell, no," one of the men said. "We talk about lots of things. Why just last week it seems to me we was talking about something else. Anybody remember what it was?"

The men laughed.

Old Bill had his chair down on all four legs, leaning forward, staring at the warden. "Hell, you should know all about hunting."

"Is that what's being talked about?"

"Sure. Hunting, that's the important thing. Putting your tag on the deer once you shoot it, that's not important at all."

"Would you trap a beaver, then throw the pelt away?"

The old man laughed. "I've done that. When I found one alive in the trap, leg not hurt much, I'd let it go."

"Why?"

"Hell, I don't know. I wasn't trapping pelts. I was trapping beaver."

"That doesn't make sense."

"Did to me. Doesn't have to make sense to you. Just did what I felt like. Man could still do that back in those days."

The warden was shaking his head. "Hunt them like deer. Then I guess you marry them and work them like horses."

An old pickup truck, with the top of the cab cut off, pulled up. A girl with dark red hair was driving. She was maybe twenty and, next to Anne, was just about the prettiest girl I'd ever seen. She waved and tapped the horn.

"That your wife?" Old Bill asked.

The warden smiled, a big smile that took all the lines out of his face. "Yes. That's my wife."

"Sometimes," the old man said, "a man'll tag one and go right on hunting. Just for the hell of it. Maybe get himself another one or two, not wanting to quit. That right?"

The warden nodded. "For some people, maybe."

"Hey, Tom!" the girl called from the pickup. "Come on!"

Old Bill jumped and peered at her. "Where you headed anyway?"

The warden hesitated. "Why, you see, she wants to drive up to the ridge. See the sun go down over the river from one of the bluffs."

"I guess there might even be a hayfield up there. You sure you already got a tag on her?"

The warden grinned and turned a little red. "I'm sure. She might argue about who put the tag on who, though." He put on his warden's wide-brimmed hat and got into the truck on the passenger's side. The girl waved and took off, doing a good job of double-clutching.

Bill stared after them. "Now there's one I'd like to go over the thank-you-ma'ams with. Puts me in mind of the redhead I chased one winter. Lived up on the ridge. Let her get away from me when she got snowed in. Somebody must've dug her out cause she got married and the next thing I knew she had herself a baby."

"Whose baby?"

"Wondered about that myself. Had a chance to look the kid over that fall at the fair. I was standing by this shake-em-up ride and there she was with the baby. She stuck him in her husband's arms, climbed into that ride and yelled, 'If he cries, tell him mama's gone to get him a milkshake.' That kid didn't look a bit like me."

"God, you must have been a hell-raiser, Bill."

"Wasn't just me. We was all hell-raisers then."

A car had roared through, the sound of it gone on down-river, but the dust still floating.

"All different now. You go racing down the road hell-bent for election, raising up a cloud so nothing's green anymore. They don't get to know this country the way we did. Hell, we could find our way around in the dark or in a snowstorm easy as buttoning up your pants with your eyes closed. Take those places I used to pick up girls, some of 'em just an old rock foundation now. Always some lilacs blooming every spring in what used to be a front yard. You know, there's nobody knows who planted those lilacs and it's not more than sixty years ago I saw smoke coming out the chimneys. Like that place I tied my horse up every Saturday night all one spring and summer. There was a big walnut tree and lilacs. By God, that was a girl, all right. I remember just how she looked. Remember just how the lilacs smelled that year. But I been trying for twenty years to remember her name and I can't."

The old man teetered back with his eyes closed. I waited, but nobody else said a word. They were all staring off in different directions. I thought about Anne. I would remember her name, all right. She wasn't like the High Ridge girl who didn't even have a name for me to forget.

The sun was getting down close to the hills on the Iowa side of the river. After the old man's talk I wasn't sure it was ever coming up again. I hitched a ride most of the way home and walked in just in time for milking.

"Where you been all day?" Erik asked.

"Hitched down to the river and bummed around."

I buried my face against the side of the cow I was milking to keep him from seeing that I was laughing. What I wanted to say was, "Day? What do you mean, day? Can't you tell I've been gone for years? How else could I be feeling like I'm the oldest man in the world?"

8

I tried looking for Anne at Elm Springs other times, but it was always the same. None of it made any sense when I tried to think about it. I had only seen her those few times. I didn't know why it could seem I was losing someone I had known all my life.

Once, the door of the shack was open. No one came when I called. I could see empty beer bottles on the table and some tin cans with their lids sticking up. As I went down the dusty path to the road, her father's clamming rig came into sight out on the river. I took one of the rowboats at the edge of the slough and rowed out.

He was laying out chains, letting them roll off the big wooden winch at the stern while he rowed. The chains had little dangles on them that the clams were supposed to grab onto when they closed their shells. He was starting to crank the chains back in when I got close. There was already a big pile of muddy clams in the bottom of the boat. The winch turned slowly, the boat moved back and the chains rattled in. Every now and then a clam would be hanging onto one of the danglers.

When he stopped to rest, I pulled alongside. He hadn't shaved for a day or two. There wasn't anything of Anne about him.

"How you doing?"

He grunted and grabbed a big clam out of a bucket. The shell was all twisted up. "Found me one just like that once. Had a big pearl inside. Sold it for fifteen hundred bucks. By God, I didn't work a lick for a year."

He turned the big clam in his hands, tracing the twisted ridges. "Means it got hurt sometime. Those kind make the pearls."

"Why don't you open it?"

He shook his head. "Always wait 'til I get to shore." His eyes flashed bright blue when he looked up from the clam. That was like Anne.

He cranked awhile. When he stopped, I asked about her.

He made me wait while he got a chew of tobacco going good. "Don't know where she's at. Cussed her out good three-four days ago for sassing me. Ain't seen her since."

He might just as well have said the world was coming to an end. On my hilltop, people didn't just go away with no one knowing what had become of them. The closest thing I could think of was when a hired man worked for us a few weeks, becoming kind of an uncle to me, then vanished, leaving me feeling lost and empty. But that wasn't anything like losing Anne.

He worked the tobacco around in his mouth and spit over the side. "Somebody thought they seen her up to La Crosse working in a restaurant. Hope they appreciate her. Ain't had a decent meal since she left."

He laughed and I wanted to shove him out of his boat and hold him under with an oar. He went on laughing, looking at me as though he knew exactly what I was thinking, his eyes bright blue the way hers had been the day our car frightened her. For a minute I had a crazy feeling there wasn't any Anne. It had been him there on the path that first day and I was lonely and had just made her up.

I shoved away from his scow. He started cranking on the winch. I could hear the chains rattling into his boat as I rowed.

I pulled hard on the oars for a few minutes until I was inside the slough, his rig out of sight. Then I let the oars drag in the dark water and tried not to think about it. The boat drifted into the shade of the willows. It was cool there, a little breeze blowing. I could hear a freight train coming, heading north toward the Twin Cities. It finally came chugging across the quiet of the slough. A Negro hobo was sitting on top one of the boxcars, singing some tune I'd never heard before, the words half lost in the clattering of the wheels across the rail joints. It was the first time I had ever seen a Negro bumming. When the train passed and the man's voice was gone, I picked up the oars and rowed to the landing.

The next Sunday, Billy and I hitched a ride to La Crosse and went around to all the restaurants we could find. A couple of times we saw girls way down the street who might have been Anne. We went running to check, but we didn't find her. By the middle of the afternoon we got tired of looking and sprawled out on the grass in a little park. Two girls kept looking us over.

"Want to move in?" Billy said.

I shook my head.

"You sure?"

"I'm sure."

He shrugged. "Well, maybe I can handle them both." He walked over and started talking with them. Pretty soon, all three looked at me. "What about him?" I heard one of the girls say.

Billy laughed. "No. He's in between girls right now." A few minutes later they got up and started away, Billy in the middle, an arm around each of them. At the edge of the park he turned and called, "Don't wait up." He laughed. "Hey, how about that? I'm in between girls, too."

I hitched a ride south on the river road in the back of a truck along with five white puppies that about licked all the skin off my face. Just before we got to Elm Springs, I pounded on the cab and asked to be let out.

I was heading for the path leading up to the shack when I saw her sitting on an overturned row boat. I ran toward her. The sun was on her hair. It wasn't Anne. The hair was red. For the first time I saw the pickup truck parked along the road.

She'd heard me running and turned around. "Hi. Going fishing?"

"No!" I almost yelled it.

"Well, I was going to warn you. The game warden's out there." She grinned. "I'm his wife."

"I know."

Her eyebrows went up.

"I was at the filling station one day when you picked him up." Her nose was peeling a little from sunburn and she wasn't wearing any makeup. She didn't seem old enough to be somebody's wife. "You were going up to look at the sunset."

She nodded and blushed a little.

"Who are you?"

"Steve Carlson." I sat down facing her, on another rowboat.

"Just bumming around?"

"I was hitching. I stopped off to see somebody." Without meaning to, I looked across the road at the shack. She noticed that.

"I hear the clammer's got a pretty daughter."

"Not any more."

"What happened?"

"She ran away."

She laughed and leaned back, hugging her knees the way Anne had done. "From him or from you?"

You can go to hell, I wanted to say to the pretty face under the mess of wind-tangled red hair. But she didn't seem to be making fun of me.

"Maybe from both of us."

"I'm sorry. I lived in a place like that, along the river. I ran away." She stared at me for a long moment. "I don't guess she would have done it because of you."

I wasn't used to people talking to me that way and I didn't know what I was supposed to say.

She was looking at the shack, something in her face different now. Then she took a deep breath and turned to me again. "What happened, anyway?"

"We had a date is all, for the excursion steamer. . . ."

I didn't mean to say it, but it all came boiling out, about Tools, Bottles and Girls, and the damned Packard, and Anne slamming the door on me.

The girl laughed and shook her head. "Oh, my. I can understand her doing that."

"Well, I can't!" I yelled. It was the first time I realized I wasn't just sad. I was angry at Anne for doing that to me.

"Where you from?"

I told her.

She nodded. "It's different along the river."

"Yeah, I know! That explains everything! 'The Devil spends extra time in a river town.' "

She smiled, looking so damned pleased with herself that I wanted to push her off the rowboat.

"I never heard that before," she said. "I like it."

"You act like it's true."

"Maybe it is. Part, anyway."

I shook my head, wanting to argue.

She leaned forward and touched my arm, looking so serious she wasn't just a pretty face anymore. "Look, you got any idea what it's like, growing up in a place like that?"

I thought of our own family, never any hitting or yelling, everyone being so damned responsible and understanding that there was no one for me to have a good stupid fight with anymore.

"I guess not."

"I do," she said. "You think you were just anybody, Steve Carlson? If I'd been her, I'd of been wishing it into something really special. How'd you expect her to feel, the way you showed up?"

"Well, who was I supposed to be?"

"A knight in shining armor riding up on a white horse, that's all."

"But it was only that once. How come she wouldn't give me another chance?"

"I don't know. I think I would've."

She was still leaning forward, looking at me closely, her face all alive with something I couldn't get hold of, and so pretty I had to keep reminding myself she was somebody's wife and too old for me. Anyway, I knew it wasn't like that. She wasn't flirting with me. I didn't know what she was doing, because I had never had a conversation like this with anyone.

"You suppose it's easy being a girl?" She was the one who sounded angry now, her eyes bright, head back.

"Hey, I'm not trying to fight with you."

"I know you're not. I'm sorry."

"It's not so damned easy being a boy, either!"

She laughed. "You've got me there. I still think it's tougher for a girl."

I didn't want to think about that. I got up from the rowboat and looked down at her. "It seems your knight on a white horse came along."

"Well," she said, "it was only a pickup truck with the cab cut off. We get wet when it rains. He's somebody special, all right."

She turned and looked out toward the river. Something ended. I didn't want to leave, because it seemed as though she actually knew Anne, better than I did. I backed away without saying anything, not sure she even realized I had gone. As I walked toward Gordon's Landing, I started missing Anne more than ever.

It was two weeks before I went to Elm Springs again. The shack was empty. Anne's father was out in that same spot with his rig so I figured the twisted up shell didn't have any pearl in it. I sat for a long time on one of the overturned rowboats watching him lay out his chains and crank them in again.

The sun was hot. No cars came by. The only sounds were the droning insects and the bubbling spring. The dry, strong smell of bergamot flowers was in the air. I let myself think of Anne, seeing the white dress, the tanned skin, the blue eyes flashing.

The sun moved behind the trees. Heat still came up from the warped boards of the rowboat, but the air was suddenly cool. A little wind came out of the north and moved along the landing, bringing a shower of yellow down from the big elm at the spring, the leaves withered from the dry heat. It had been a long time since the night of the excursion steamer and the man at French Prairie who had maybe just made up the other half of himself.

A stronger gust ran along the shore. The yellow leaves floated down all around me, some falling onto the water and skimming along the surface. I got up from the rowboat, took a long drink from the rusty can at the spring, and walked up the path toward the shack. When I yelled "Goodbye!" my voice bounced off the wall of the bluff and echoed back and forth a few times.

I didn't look for Anne after that. Summer was getting away. I couldn't wait any longer to find some part of me that was lost there at Elm Springs.

9

*U*p in the ridge-top world of the farm, life went right on as though nothing had happened. No one stared at me and said I looked different. They didn't even seem to know this summer wasn't just like all the other summers.

After breakfast on Monday I helped Mom wash the milk things, thinking practically out loud all the questions I had rattling around inside, about Anne, the man at French Prairie, all the talk about men and women at the station in Gordon's Landing. Every time I had a question ready, something closed down inside and she didn't hear me. That had never happened before, her not knowing what I was thinking and no way to move across the silence to each other. Each time I put a milk pail down I let the bail crash against the side, wanting to hear the noise, and I watched her and wondered. If it was with men and women the way it sounded at the station, how come she and Dad still looked at each other sometimes as though the rest of us weren't there? What was she thinking about as her hands did the work by themselves and she looked out across the ridges at something that I couldn't see?

She went right on working and didn't hear a word I was thinking, but just as we finished put her hand on my shoulder and said "You seem far away."

The ground stayed dry. No matter how much Dad watched the horizon and talked about rain, no rain came. He kept talking about it being a funny year. "Sure is," I would say, laughing inside because he didn't have any idea what was funny about the year for me.

A neighbor came by and he and Dad stood looking across the road, telling each other how dry it was and that the heat was going to ruin the oats because the heads were in the milk stage and would ripen too fast and turn to chaff.

I listened to them, laughing again, wanting to say, "Can that happen to people, too?"

Seventeen-year locusts filled the heat with their dry screaming. I raced as fast as I could along the narrow paths when I brought in the cows, running them too fast, udders swinging, milk squirting out, first one side, then the other.

Even at noon, when the others were resting, I would run off into the woods, then run back, covered with sweat, bringing a few wildflowers, so no one would ask questions.

Every day I checked the apples on the Tetawsky tree, beginning to turn gold, ripening too early, like the oats. I would reach up, and stand with a smooth apple in my hand, remembering the three of us fighting over the biggest ones, testing them so often they were covered with dark bruises from our thumbs.

Once in the early evening I went down the hillside to the log cabin Erik and I had built. I started a fire in the stove, then went outside and sat in a grove of poplars, watching the smoke come out the stovepipe. I waited below the rattling leaves, but a younger me didn't come walking out the door. Erik didn't appear. It wasn't *our* cabin anymore. The first year Erik went to high school we had a big fight and I sold my half of the cabin to him. He spent a lot of time there that fall, sitting for hours on the doorstep, smoking a corncob pipe and looking around as though he was expecting somebody. I watched from the woods, waiting to see who was supposed to come. The next fall Erik told me I could have the cabin back and he never went there after that.

When I got back to the house, I undressed in the dark and lay staring at the ceiling, listening to the windmill trying to pump water in the light breeze, the big wheel creaking around slowly, slowly, the sound faster on the downstroke, slowing on the upstroke, and each time I hung suspended with it, wanting to run out and push it across dead center and get it over with.

By Friday night I couldn't stand it anymore. Right after chores I ran down into the woods toward the flat rock, crashing through the brush, sending stones rolling ahead of me. I climbed the sheer side, pulling myself up with my hands. When my head came over the edge, the first thing I saw was Bottles, reading a book and drinking from a bottle of beer. There were three empties and two full ones beside him. He held one out, never raising his eyes from the book. "Here you go, Steve. Still cold."

I pulled myself up, angry at finding him on my rock. "What the hell you doing here?"

He waved the bottle toward the valley, still reading. "Keeping away from the tigers."

"As Girls would say, you're getting complicated."

He drained the bottle and lifted it, then looked at me for the first time. "Here's to Girls, where the hell ever he is."

"What does that mean?"

"Got off the boat with that girl wearing a dress made out of old wallpaper, never came back."

"What about the tigers?"

Bottles swung his arm way back and threw the empty bottle, the mouth making a deep, tumbling whistle in the air. It crashed a long way below. He cupped his hands to his mouth and yelled. "Come out and fight, Goddamned Tigers!"

The echoes kept saying tigers, tigers, tigers for what seemed like ten minutes.

"Know why they won't come out?"

I shook my head.

He opened the last beer, took a long pull, then banged himself on the chest with the bottle until foam ran down his shirt. "Because maybe we're tigers, too. That's why they won't come out."

"You're getting even more complicated. A little drunk, too."

He turned the pages of the book to a map and held it out to me. Toward one edge of the map, all the towns and roads ended. The rest was labeled "Unexplored," and there was a fierce-looking animal and some words in another language.

Bottles pointed to the words. "Genuine Latin. Know what the book says that says? Tell you what the book says that says. 'Beyond Here There Be Tigers.' What you think of that?"

I looked out over the valley. The sky was a deep red to the west, bright gold overhead. A little wind blew along the ravine, moving in waves across the grass of the empty meadow, turning it from red to gold to red. The bats were already flying. Suddenly the tigers were there, tails switching as they paced back and forth in the shadows near the trees. They were watching us and I wanted to run home, jump into bed and pull the covers over my head.

Bottles nudged me. "I said, what you think?"

"I think I'll push you off this damn rock and let the tigers have you!"

Bottles looked down, hair swinging in front of his face. "Can't see 'em." He wagged a finger at me. "If a tiger chases you in a dream, know what you're supposed to do?"

I shook my head.

"Supposed to stop running, turn around, ask him what he wants."

I had a sudden picture of doing that and I laughed. "Hey, Bottles, you think tigers know what girls are for?"

"They don't know. Tigers're from before thinking about sex got invented." He thumped the book. "Too dark or could show you. In old days, everybody identical. 'Til these two babies, one with a peg in its crotch, one with a slit. Consternation! Nobody could figure what it meant. Asked a wise old man. Man said, 'The peg is to hang the world on. So that one'll own the world. Slit belongs. . . .' "

I wasn't hearing him anymore. I sipped at the beer, thinking about things going on without me in the different world of the valley and realized I'd been feeling about thirteen years old all week. The sunset colors were almost gone, the air cooler all at once, the rocks still warm from the day and a funny dry smell of lichens coming up. The leaves on a stunted white oak, growing up out of a split in the rock, were half brown and rattling in a breeze coming up out of the valley.

Bottles finished his beer and stretched out on his back. "You think tigers have maps? You think maybe their maps say 'Beyond here there be humans?' "

He stopped talking. His empty bottle rolled along the flat rock into the split where the little white oak was growing. His eyes were closed. I left him there and went back through the dark woods to the farm.

10

Saturday night I started out with Lars and Erik, not even knowing where they were going. I had to go someplace. At Three Points, only four miles from home, they got together with their own stag gang. One of the others had a brand-new car and I knew what that meant. They would all pile into it, taking some beer with them, and spend the night going around to see which steep hills the car could climb in high gear. Because of that, Lars and Erik said I could have our car for the night.

"If you get home early," Lars said.

"And don't drive fast or go very far," Erik said.

"But if you do, disconnect the speedometer cable."

"And stay out of trouble."

"And stay out of the back seat," Lars said, grinning, but I was sure he didn't know about the night in High Ridge.

I didn't even look for anybody else, just drove out the long ridge and down into the river valley. When I stopped at the filling station in Gordon's Landing, the usual gang was there.

"Well the best one was when that George somebody and. . . ."

"You mean George Williams."

"Yeah. Him and that skinny girl he'd been going with about nine years, they was parked, as usual. And this truck ran smack into the rear end of George's car. Well don't you just know there was legs'n clothes flying all over the place. Best yet was when the paper came out and the editor he wrote that the car was hit so hard that George and his passenger got thrown into the back seat."

The old man noticed me for the first time.

"Hey, there Boy. You ever find that girl you lost?"

I had to stop and remember that he meant the one at High Ridge. I shook my head. "I lost another one since then."

"The hell you say?" He nodded. "I was always doing that, losing one while I chased me another one. What was her name, the last one?"

"Anne."

"Nope. That wasn't it."

"Billy around?"

"Been working across the river in Iowa a couple weeks."

That started a discussion about whether or not Iowa girls were different from Wisconsin girls with everything running in the same direction. I left, thinking about going past Elm Springs again, but turned south along the river instead, shadflies thick ahead of the car lights.

I stopped at a place called The Hole in the Wall. It stood close against one of the hills, with the road and slough right in front, the railroad tracks and river out beyond. The car crunched over empty beer cans when I drove in. I got out and leaned against the hood, liking the idea of people seeing me with a car. Shadflies were wrecking themselves against the windows and around the light above the door. When they had used themselves up, they fell in a black layer on the three concrete steps. A fat, wheezing man waddled out to sweep them away, but he couldn't keep ahead of them.

"To hell with it," he said, putting the broom down beside the steps. He saw me watching. "Go ahead, track 'em in. Make the floor good and slippery for dancing."

The jukebox kept playing over and over again a song called "It Makes no Difference Now." I could hear voices coming from parked cars and every now and then a beer can would fly out a window and roll along the ground.

Something white began moving between the cars, whirling and flashing like one of the light-crazy shadflies. A boy and a girl were dancing, a million miles from anywhere. Now and then a head bobbed up in a back seat, a face stared out at them, then sank back again.

The white dress floated away from the boy and moved toward the door. He came after her and I saw it was a boy I knew at school.

I stepped toward them. "Hey, Pete. Want me to catch her for you?"

She was laughing, looking over her shoulder at him. Then she stopped and was quiet and cool. I couldn't see her face. Pete came after her sweating and breathing hard. He tried to put his arm around her and she slid away from him. He followed, his feet clattering the beer cans, and reached for her again, but his hand stopped. He was weaving and his hair had that tousled look it got when he started drinking too early in the evening.

"You're never going to make it to midnight," I said.

He grinned, still looking at her, one hand reaching.

A sharp light caught us there. We turned and the beam held us motionless, then swept away. It was a river boat, its light searching along the shore for range marks. I could see the running lights as it rode the current downstream toward the locks and then on down the river to God knew where with its line of empty barges.

The jukebox paused for a minute. In the quiet I could hear the hum of the boat's diesels. The light found us again and the girl took a deep breath. Before the light swept away, I really saw her. The coolness was just a trick of blond hair, white dress and motionlessness. Her lips were open a little, there was a quick pulse beating at the side of her throat and she was not just cool.

"I don't know who you are," I said.

The light moved downstream. I watched it go with the empty feeling I always got when a lighted up train went by or a river boat headed out of sight, going somewhere beyond the little bit of country I had seen.

"Elaine," she said.

Her face was in darkness again, but she was looking at me. She took Pete's arm and then my arm and turned us so that we walked as a unit of three to the steps. Even though we ducked in quickly, a flock of shad-flies came with us and one landed on the shoulder of Elaine's dress. It was still there when we got to a booth. While Pete went to get the drinks, I picked up the shadfly by its lacy wings and held it out to her. She opened my fingers and it fell halfway to the floor, then spread its wings and joined others, whirling around the dim light above us.

Pete took Elaine's arm and pulled her out of the booth onto the dance floor. That was when I first noticed how good her legs were, rounded in the right place and tapering down to slim ankles. She was all right in front, too, not bulging out at the world but there just the same and you didn't have to wait until she stood just right before you could see them.

I watched Pete and Elaine dancing, thinking of the way we spoke about girls at school, everybody sounding as though they had been to bed with hundreds of them. For some reason we never talked about what made a girl good-looking; or not good-looking. They were just one or the other and we knew which the minute we saw them. I watched Elaine and wondered if I would remember her just from knowing how she looked. Or would I have to feel her fingers loosening mine to let the shadfly go, or get to know how she felt in my arms in a parked car and then I would always know her. Maybe that was why the Oldest Man in the World couldn't remember the name of the girl who had lived out on Sand Creek. Her name didn't have anything to do with it.

I tried to memorize Elaine. She had blond hair, almost gold color, down to her shoulders, blue eyes and a slim face, lips full and everything in her face definite so that I didn't have to add anything myself to make her whole. I could tell she was Norwegian, but she had a quick way of moving and doing things with her hands that made her seem more like a dark-haired, Irish girl.

I realized the same song was playing again for about the eighty-ninth time. "Makes no difference now/what kind of life they hand me./I'll get along without you now/that's plain to see./There was something had to happen/and it happened somehow./I don't worry,/'cause it makes no difference now."

I started thinking about Anne and got that rabbit-jumped-over-my-grave cold feeling. It was the damn song, the sad kind that sounds totally familiar the first time you ever hear it.

I went over to the jukebox. Two boys were standing there laughing. "What the hell's going on?"

"It's stuck," one of them said.

"Well can't somebody unstick it?"

"Fatso opened the thing up and tried."

"Well who played that one in the first place?"

He pointed to the bar. "Some drunk guy."

There was something familiar about the way the person was hunched over his drink. I moved closer and got a look at his face in the mirror. It was Bottles. He was quietly singing along with the jukebox. "It was just a year ago/that I first met you./I learned to love you/and I thought you loved me, too./Now that all is in the past/and I'll get by somehow./I don't worry,/'cause it makes no difference now."

"Hey, Bottles, did you really play that damn song?"

"Of course."

"Why?"

"Because it goes so well with beer and with my sad and lonely life."

"My God, I think you're still drunk from yesterday."

"Yesterday? I wasn't drunk yesterday. Hey, Steve. You know those tires we roll down the hill — guess what's painted now on the cardboards we put inside?"

"Tigers," I said.

Pete and Elaine danced near us, Elaine looking cool and aloof, Pete sweating and having trouble with his feet. She waved.

"She with you?" Bottles asked.

"Mostly I'm in between girls. But if Pete has a couple more beers, maybe I'm with her."

"What happened to the other one?"

"What other one?"

"Elm Springs girl. Prettiest girl you ever saw. That's what you said."

I smiled, remembering that day when Billy Wallin drove me up to see her. "Well she is the prettiest girl I ever saw. Or was. She wouldn't have anything to do with me after that night. She went away some place."

Bottles was staring at me, all round-eyed like an owl. "Still think about her?"

"I guess so. I never found out anything about her."

He laughed. "Sure. That's how it is."

"She wasn't playing games with me."

"Maybe it was you." Bottles carefully put his beer down on the bar. "Tell you a story. About a dead Roman. Which is the next most pres-tig-igious thing to being a dead Greek. Mike the Angel. Hell of a painter. Statues, too. One statue's called David, alive almost. S'got a chip out of one foot. Know how it got that chip?"

Bottles poked me. I shook my head.

"Tell you how. When Mike the Angel finished the Goddamned thing he felt like a father. Stepped back and whacked that Goddamned David on the foot with a hammer and yelled 'Speak!' "

Bottles stood up and shouted, "SPEAK!" Everybody in the place turned around. The big, wheezing bartender pulled him back onto his stool.

Bottles waved a finger at me. "Get it?"

People were still watching us. I shook my head.

"You made her up."

I remembered her on the path with the birds flying around her. "No I didn't."

"You hit her on the foot, said speak, and she didn't speak."

"Damnit, Bottles! You're crazy!"

"Nope. You make somebody up and fall in love. So who're you in love with?"

I just stared at him.

"Sure," Bottles said. "Like the man at French Prairie that night. Did I tell you Girls still didn't come home?"

"What the hell are you talking about?"

Bottles grinned. "Somebody cut us in two once. Halves of an apple. Spend the rest of our life trying to find the other half."

He sat there smiling at me, face all relaxed. I got off the stool. If I stayed there I was going to hit him with his own beer bottle. "It Makes no Difference Now" ended and started again. Pete went crashing out the door letting in a whole flock of shadflies and Elaine came up and touched my arm. We started dancing. I could see Bottles watching us. He stood up and bowed, spilling some of his beer. "Hit her on the foot," he yelled.

Elaine laughed. "What's he talking about?"

"He thinks I'm making you up."

"Are you?"

I thought about Anne again. "I don't know."

She looked at me, head tilted to one side. "There are things I don't know about you."

"There are things nobody ever knows about anybody." It sounded so much like something Bottles would say that I started laughing.

There were shadflies all around the dancefloor light. One came down and landed on Elaine's hair.

"You're wearing a black lace cap," I said, flipping it away. The way she looked gave me a crazy feeling I had said "I love you." She put her head on my shoulder and every minute or so she'd glance up, smiling a little, reminding me she was there. She didn't have to remind me. I wanted to hold her close, but I felt eight years old at the school party, not able to remember my lines because I didn't know if I was all buttoned up.

Finally I said "Elaine. . . ." She looked up, waiting, all motionlessness again and I couldn't remember what I was going to say. After a minute I asked how old she was.

"Sixteen."

Maybe it was pure chance but I'd never done anything like that before. Without even thinking about it I said, "And your birthday is August sixteenth."

She stopped dancing. "Pete told you."

She wouldn't believe me when I said he hadn't, so I just said it was because I had known her for a long time and I would have to come see her on her birthday. August sixteenth was only a little more than a month away.

"All right," she said, taking a deep breath.

Pete came back, followed by a swarm of shadflies, and stood by the door, teetering.

"Are you still with him?" I asked.

"I don't know yet."

"I'll be here if you need a way home."

Pete saw us and pulled her away. I went back to the bar, ordered a beer and watched Bottles who was singing along with the jukebox again. After a couple of minutes I decided I wasn't mad at him anymore and moved up beside him. "Bottles, if you say one more word about me making anybody up, I'll hit you with this beer bottle."

A big smile flashed onto his face. He looked so happy to see me I felt bad for ever leaving him.

"Don't have to talk about that," he said. "I can talk about anything, especially if it's not important. What about. . . .?"

"No Tigers, either," I said.

"All right." He looked around the room. The shadflies were yo-yoing up and down at the lights, flying up, parachuting down two or three feet, then flying up again in some kind of a pattern. "Shadflies," Bottles said. "Called that because shadfish eat them. And what do shadflies eat? Nothing. They don't even have a mouth?"

"Everything has a mouth."

"Nope. When they're worms or something under the water, yeah. But not the flies."

"How do they live without a mouth."

"They don't live. Die in one day or so, all of them. Breed first, lay eggs. So who needs to live longer than that? Birth, copulation, egg laying and death, that's all. You suppose they get a whole life squeezed into one day? You suppose the old ones, wings all ragged and weak, talk to each other about the good old days?"

I thought about the Oldest Man in the World. "Sure. Some old one's saying right now 'Hey, remember that young thing I met way back about nine o'clock this morning? What ever happened to her? Think she laid those eggs I helped her with? Anybody remember what her name was?' "

"We forgot something," Bottles said. "They can't talk. They don't have any mouths."

"Oh, well let's talk about something else anyway." We both watched Pete trying to dance with Elaine. Bottles looked at me and raised an eyebrow.

"No," I said.

"All right. What about them?" He pointed.

It was another couple, a tall boy who looked as if somebody had hit him over the head one too many times, and a good-looking girl who was staring off into space. We called them "the going steady couple." Neither of them ever danced with anybody else and they never seemed to speak to each other.

"Nobody there," I said.

"Talked to him once," Bottles said. "Told me he was stuck with her, couldn't make out, couldn't let go. Said she'd be gone forever. He might never find anybody like her again."

Bottles stood up. "I know! Let's give them a decent funeral." He clapped his hands until quite a few people were watching. He crossed himself. "Bless you my children. Go now into that great nothingness you love so well."

There was some laughter and applause, but mostly people looked puzzled. The going steady couple went on dancing, moving like puppets, their faces exactly the way they had been before.

"Too late," I said. "They can't hear you."

Bottles sat down again. "I guess it wouldn't do any good to hit them on the feet either. All right, another subject. A map."

"I said no tigers."

"Different map. Game of X's map."

"What's that?"

"Not going to tell you. Not finished. Never be finished, come to think of it. Every night more X's. Indispensible map for males who hunt females."

I looked for Elaine and saw her at the booth alone, seeming lost in the noise and jostling of the place. I went over to her. "Where's Pete?"

"You were right. He didn't make it to midnight."

"He's not going to take you home?"

"He's not even going to take himself home."

"Where is he?"

"Somebody's driving him."

"What about you?"

"They offered me a ride." She smiled a little. "I said I thought I had a way home."

We started dancing and now it was all different because she wasn't just Elaine. She was Anne in her white dress. She was the red-headed wife of the warden. She was all the women the men talked about at the filling station. She was the girl at High Ridge. She was with me and for once I had a car waiting outside. I pulled her and she came up close, moving against me, my right hand feeling the outline of a strap under her dress in back, my fingers wanting to follow it up over her shoulder and down. When she finally pulled back a little to look at me, her face very still, I realized my mind had been turned off, not even noticing that the same music was still playing over and over.

I'd only had two beers but something funny was going on inside my head. I kept looking at her, my fingertips on the strap under her dress, a voice inside my head saying over and over, "Her name is Elaine." I could imagine the Oldest Man in the World wonder about that, then shake his head.

I pulled her close again, but Bottles was watching us from the bar. I didn't want him to do a funeral service for us, so we danced with some space between us.

The jukebox stopped and didn't start again. The fat man was standing beside it. He banged on the wall with a beer bottle until he got everybody shut up.

"Now Goddamnit, listen to me! I just got a tip. The damned State men are out, checking ages. Anybody who ain't twenty-one get the hell out of here."

That was just about all of us. Usually age made no difference because the county sheriff didn't seem to care. But State men were different.

Elaine was holding on to my arm and all at once looked about twelve. I saw Bottles watching us, by himself now at the bar. "Hey, Bottles. I know you're a thousand years old. You want a ride home anyway?"

He got up, carrying a bottle of beer and something down at his side in the other hand. People started asking me for rides. I agreed to take two other couples and we shoved through the mob hanging outside the door. The fat man was wheezing and coughing, wet all over with sweat and trying to move people away with the same broom he'd used for the shadflies.

"Nothing illegal about being outside!" a boy yelled.

The fat man grabbed a bottle out of the boy's hand. "There is when you're drinking beer. Get the hell out of here!"

Bottles held the car door open for Elaine. When I got in on the other side, he was still standing there looking at us. "Goodbye," he said.

"I thought you were going with us."

"I am."

"Aw, come on, Bottles. Let's get out of here."

"All right." He got in beside Elaine but stayed clear over next to the door.

I pulled out, over a new layer of beer cans. There were people yelling at us, sticking their thumbs up, some already walking toward Gordon's Landing. Elaine stayed close to me. The next time I looked at Bottles, I couldn't see his face, just a dark shadow with a funny yellow glow coming out around it. I flipped the overhead light on and then off. He had a big, fat book up close to his face and his cigarette lighter going.

"For God's sake Bottles, what are you reading now?"

"*The Decline and Fall of the Roman Empire,* Volume Two," he said, not looking up.

"You got to be kidding," one of the girls in the back seat said.

Bottles turned slowly to look at her. "Properly speaking, only goats kid."

A boy laughed. "Any sex in it?"

"Sure. It's just one long rape scene."

"It *is*?"

"Sure. But you wouldn't be interested. It's rape rather more on a cultural level."

Bottles peered out around the book, looking like a big fat owl in the glow from the cigarette lighter. "Anyone like to discuss cultural rape?"

"I'd like to discuss just about any kind of rape," the same boy said.

Elaine was sitting up very straight on the seat.

"Aw, cut it out, everybody," I said. "It's a history book."

"Sure it is," Bottles said. "I wonder if they played the game in ancient Rome. You suppose there are places along the Tiber where they put X's on the maps for personal conquests? You think that's what Shakespeare meant when he said 'Have all thy conquests, triumphs, spoils shrunk to this small measure?' "

"What are you talking about?" Elaine asked.

"Sex," Bottles said. "It accounts for the hump on the back of the camel and the Sphinx's inscrutable smile."

Elaine moved a little closer to me and Bottles began reading again.

I knew what kind of a night it was going to be. There were seven of us in the car, all living in different places. I reached under the dash and unscrewed the speedometer cable, remembering something Erik had said once. "There's just no sense getting in a discussion with Dad about how can you possibly put a hundred miles on the car going someplace five miles from home."

I started asking the two couples questions, trying to figure out a route that wouldn't take all night, then drove where they told me, waiting at intersections for a head to raise up, figure out where we were and tell me which way to turn.

The first girl lived along a creek, in a narrow hollow, so dark I couldn't see anything at first when I stopped and turned the lights out, but a rattling sound told me there was a cottonwood tree in the yard. As my eyes got used to the darkness, I could see a house close against the hillside. I put my hand on Elaine's shoulder while we waited. For a minute she tilted her head, her cheek warm against my hand. The crickets started up. I could hear the sound of water going down over a riffle.

The boy came back and we headed for the next drop-off, climbing to the high ridge. It was cooler there, with the sweet smell of growing corn mixing with the smell of dust. The girl reached from the back seat, touched my shoulder and told me where to turn. She left her hand there. It was the first time I had thought about any of them except as couples. I couldn't see her face and didn't even remember what she looked like.

"There," she said, and I turned onto a farm driveway. "Remember," she said, "it's the first right past the school if you ever do this again."

She gave my shoulder a little squeeze and got out. Elaine was looking straight ahead and I didn't know if she had noticed.

I had pulled up beside a squeaking windmill. The water was running through a pipe, splashing into one end of a stock tank and running right out again over the top at the other end. I could smell the wetted dust.

We waited a long time. The other boy kept looking at the dark farmhouse. "He's taking his own sweet time. Didn't take me that long." He laughed. "But then they say she's the girl who changed neck from a noun to a verb."

Elaine moved out from under my hand. Bottles was still reading, the cigarette lighter getting dimmer.

The boy came back and we started out again. When we stopped to let him out, all I could see was a garage door in the car lights, covered with license plates, some of them old and rusty. The last boy got out beside a mailbox and walked away. He could have lived in a cave for all I ever knew. Bottles crawled into the back seat and lay down.

I had been trying to talk to Elaine. I found out she lived on a farm, that they had dairy cows, raised tobacco and that her older brothers drank quite a bit. She told me she still had two years in high school, a different one than mine, and I told her I was a year ahead of her. That seemed to use up everything we had to say. Whenever I glanced at her, she smiled, looking very pretty. Every time I wanted to reach out for her I started remembering the time I undressed an old doll of Mom's to see what I could find under the clothes. My brothers caught me at it. They laughed and said it wasn't any use, that they had already checked, and I could find out more by looking at the underwear and corset ads in the mail-order catalogs.

Elaine told me where to turn onto a narrow road with brush on both sides. The farm buildings sat at the upper end of a ravine, hidden until the very last minute.

A dog came to meet us. Elaine leaned out the window and spoke. It trotted alongside and quit barking, but it had done its work. A cow bawled a couple of times and a rooster was trying out the idea of crowing.

I pulled up under a pine tree and turned out the lights. The dog put its front paws on the door, licked her arm and stared at us.

"My God," I said. "What does he do, report to your parents in the morning?"

Elaine laughed. "He just wants his ears scratched." She did that and the dog left us. We sat listening to the sleepy rooster. Finally he gave up. I tried to think of something to say. Elaine's head was resting back against the seat. I wanted to reach out for her, but when I moved, something changed in her face. Bottles muttered in his sleep and the rear seat squeaked. I got out and opened the door for her.

We stood under the pine tree, waiting. The moon had come up and a few white clouds were moving very slowly beyond the top of the tree, the wind making that soft sighing that comes only from a white pine.

I heard Elaine take a deep breath as she looked up at the tree. "We used to take pillows up there. We'd curl around the trunk and read. Or maybe sleep." She sounded surprised as though it was something she'd done a long time ago and had forgotten until now.

"Hey, we did the same thing in our yard. I supposed we were the only ones."

I pictured her climbing up the tree, holding a pillow, the wind pushing her clothes against her. I thought about climbing up there with her. I thought about being down below looking up at her as she climbed. The skirt of her white dress moved in the wind. I went closer, wanting to touch her, and put my hands on her hair, lifting it from her shoulders, letting it fan out in the breeze.

"That feels nice and cool." She shivered and turned her head, the way she had in the car so her cheek was warm against the inside of my wrist.

Her hair, looking almost white in the faint light, ran through my fingers and fell back to her shoulders, little waves of motion still going through it. I couldn't wait any longer. I put my hands on the warmth of her face, gave her a little pull and I was kissing her and she was kissing me back, that voice somewhere inside me saying "Oh, my God! Oh, my God!"

She pulled back first, looked up and took a deep breath. I could feel her shaking. Her lips were apart, the moon shining from above and a little to one side leaving her face half in light, half in shadow, like an Old World painting. Something about it stopped me. It wasn't the way it had been in High Ridge when I had an ultimate in the back seat with me and didn't know what to do next. I just didn't know what was going on because I kept looking at her, thinking maybe this is the last time I will see her, so real and isolated from everything else.

I shook my head. "What the hell are you doing to me?"

"I'm not doing anything to you."

She put her arms on my shoulders. I pulled her close and we just held each other.

After a long time, she pulled away and bowed her head against me. I could hear her breathing. The wind played with her hair and I heard the sound of the tree again and could smell the sweet, sticky fragrance of the pitch.

She took my hand and led me toward the door, laughing when I stumbled over the dog who was sprawled across the walk. By the time I got straightened up she had slipped inside and was looking at me through the screendoor.

"Elaine, come out a minute."

She shook her head.

"What's the matter? Afraid of me?"

"Of course."

If she had laughed as she said it, I would have wanted to tear the screendoor off the hinges, but her voice was quiet, almost matter of fact.

"All right, but if I come back next Saturday night, will you come out?"

She smiled and her hair moved, shining in the dim light as she nodded. "Goodnight, Steve."

It was the first time I had heard her say my name. I stood looking at her with my mouth open and she moved back from the door, out of the moonlight and was gone. There wasn't a sound from the dark, sleeping house.

I started back to the car, falling over the damn dog again. He looked up at me, his tail thumping against the stones of the walk. I would have sworn he was smiling and I half expected him to say "Goodnight, Steve."

I got the car started and made it out of the driveway all right. At the main road I had to stop and think for about five minutes before I could remember where I was and which way to turn for home.

At breakfast the next morning I suddenly realized Mom had answered the phone and was looking at me. "Did you see anything of Bottles last night?"

"Sure, I gave him a ride."

"Well, his father says he never got home. They need him for the haying."

I started easing my chair back. "Ah, I guess he must still be out in the car."

It felt as though several thousand people at the table had turned to stare at me. Dad spilled coffee onto his pancakes. "What are you talking about?"

"I'll go take him home," I said and got out of there.

I woke Bottles and said I'd drive him, but he opened the door and climbed out. "Thank you very much. I'd rather walk through the dewey fields of morning."

He walked away, reading the book as he went.

I saw something shiny on the back seat. "Hey, you forgot your lighter."

He waved his hand, still reading. "That's all right. It needs filling anyway."

I went back to the house and started eating again, with Dad's eyes boring into me. When I thought he was about ready to let go, I tried to beat him to it.

"Do you know," I said to Mom who was looking amused about the whole thing, "that he's right now walking across the field reading a book. And what do you suppose he's reading?"

"I couldn't guess."

"*The Decline and Fall of the Roman Empire.*"

She nodded. "That sounds like a good early morning book."

"Bottles says . . ."

Dad's hand banged down on the table. "I just don't understand how you could forget something like that."

I thought about the old leather suitcase with all those pictures of him when he was young. "You just don't remember."

He misunderstood, which was probably just as well, and said, "Well next time, you remember!"

11

Monday was another hot, dry, endless day in the hayfields. Last Saturday night and Elaine seemed a long time ago. Next Saturday night and Elaine seemed far away. The woods were already half dark when I took the cows down the lane after milking, herded them into the lower pasture and closed the gate. A vesper sparrow was singing on the lowest wire of the fence. Something stirred in the shadows under a big oak tree and the sparrow flew, white tail feathers flashing.

"Hello, Steve."

It was Bottles, sitting back against the trunk, some of the sunset color on his face.

"You look like an Indian," I said.

"Sure. Didn't I ever tell you?"

"I never know when to believe you."

"That's all right. Neither do I."

I started to sit down beside him.

"Watch out for the empties."

I might have known. He had beer with him, in a paper bag in his lap. I had to move three empty bottles before I could sit down.

"You celebrating something?"

"Wanted to tell you goodbye."

"You keep saying that. You going away?"

"Not me."

"What're you talking about?"

"You and Elaine."

He tipped his head way back, turned a beer bottle upside down over his open mouth and let it gurgle away until it was empty. "Don't play the game of X's with her."

"Bottles, I don't know what you're talking about."

He smoothed out the bare ground in front of us, pushing aside the old leaves, the acorns and their caps. With a twig he drew an outline in the dust and added crooked lines. "Map of the county. With roads."

He began adding X's. "X at Hole in the Wall parking lot. X at entrance to fairgrounds. X at turnout on Long Hill. One at Elm Springs. X at these intersections. At the parks. All the gravel quarries. Schoolyards. Graveyards. Know what happens all those places?"

I shook my head.

"Tell you what happens all those places. Cars park, at night. Could show that map to men all over the Goddamned county, they'd know what it is. Bastards'd get all choked up remembering those warm bodies."

"I guess you're right. The Oldest Man in the World would know, all right."

Bottles traced in another road and held the twig poised. "Want to put an X at Elaine's house?"

"No!"

He erased that road. "OK, not yet."

I didn't know if I wanted to laugh or cry. Using my finger, I put in an X for the cheese factory at High Ridge. "You forgot some."

"Sure. New ones all the time."

"That's just plain dumb, Bottles. That's no game!"

"Not through yet."

He drew an outline of a person in the dust, and put an X on the mouth, X's on the legs, bigger X's for each breast, and a very big one at the crotch.

"There. Every X on the Goddamned map's got a body goes with it. Object of game — proceed to proper location and achieve progression to the Big X."

"A boy at High Ridge calls that the third ultimate."

"Sure. One man's third ultimate's another man's Big X. So step right up. Many tries as you want. Doesn't always start first night. With some girls, forget what you're doing. Start thinking she's people. Land on that square, go back to start. Lose your turn, some other bastard gets your turn. Maybe go back to different girl, start over. Same thing, though. One night kiss, next night legs, next halfway legs to Big X, breast number one through cloth, breast number two no cloth, then Big X, then Big X with your Big X."

Bottles finished another beer. "Know what the trouble with damn game is?"

"How the hell much beer did you start out with?"

"Ten bottles. Magic number. Egyptians like seven. Indians like four. I like ten. Like beer even better. Got another bottle in the spring for going home. Tell you what the trouble is. No place to go from Big X."

"I thought that was winning."

"Ah-ha! What everybody thinks. Real object, find out which way going to lose. Like getting almost to Big X with your Big X. Night after night. Get almost there, then not do it. Spend all night not doing it.

"Another way to lose. Run out of X's. Big X with your Big X every night. Nobody left. Game over without ending, or ending without over. Get sick of her. Go back to start. Find some girl not explored yet. Little X's to Big X all over again."

"Bottles, how the hell do you think up this stuff? You're crazy!"

"Nicest thing anybody ever said."

He reached over to pat me on the shoulder and annointed me with beer.

"S'different sometimes. Get interrupted. Put in a bookmark. Talk to her, even. But just goes faster second time, right past the bookmark."

He laughed. "Hey, Steve, how about that? Finish reading her in three weeks'r pay five cents a day."

I finished my third beer. I could see lamplight from the house a quarter of a mile away. The beer drinking and the conversation seemed strange that close to home. I looked at the outline of the body with the X's.

"It's not Elaine."

"Not yet."

It wasn't anybody. Except that it was partly the girl at High Ridge.

Bottles was trying to pound an acorn into the mouth of a bottle and the beer was foaming out around it. "You think girls got maps, too? You think they got bodies of boys with X's?"

"Hey," I said, "you keep talking like some kind of studhorse expert and I never even saw you with a girl."

"Only when I was young."

"For God's sake, how old are you now?"

"Very, very old. Twenty, almost. Going on fifty-nine."

I started to laugh, then decided he was right. He did seem old. "So how come you don't take out girls now?"

"Already told you. Poke them with your ultimate, yell 'speak.' They don't speak anymore than when you hit them on the foot. Either you do it and she goes away, or don't do it and she goes away. Either she's there and gone. Or she's not there and gone."

"What?"

"I couldn't stand how lonely it was."

Bottles turned the paper bag inside out to make sure there was no beer in it. He tried to pick up the empties but kept dropping them. He handed me the bag and I began picking them up.

"What you think of the game?" he said.

"I don't like it!"

"Nothing to do with it. Got to play. Think you won't? Play anyway, no matter what you think."

"Damnit, Bottles! I don't want to hear anymore about it!"

He watched me while I gathered up the bottles, head nodding up and down loosely like one of those silly dolls with heads on a spring in the back window of a car. I could smell the dust with the beginning wetness of dew on it, the smell of growing corn and sweet clover blooming along the fence rows.

Bottles began counting on the fingers of his left hand. "Let's see. No Tigers. No Elaine. No X's. Guess you want me not to say goodbye anymore either."

"That's right!"

He pulled himself up, using the tree trunk. I handed him the bag of bottles and he walked away. Only it seemed the other way around, with me walking away from him, even if I was still sitting with my back against the tree.

"Hey, Bottles!"

He stopped and moved his feet about ten times to get turned around.

"Once, maybe four or five years ago, I found some potatoes cooking, up on top of the big flat rock. Did you leave them there?"

"No."

"Well, somebody did."

"Haven't lived here that long. Anyway, potatoes are not a life force." He waved the bag of bottles. "Goodbye, Steve."

He crashed through the brush, muttering and swearing. I could tell exactly when he went too far left and got into the blackberries, when he hit the barberry bush and when he forgot about the barbed-wire fence. The bottles kept crashing when he fell down. Each time there was a long silence and I knew he was feeling around in the darkness for them, then the sound of him fighting his way through the brush again.

I started laughing and couldn't stop. I imagined him trying to get that last bottle of beer and falling into the spring. I figured he would scream when he hit that cold water. I stopped laughing and listened. Whippoorwills were calling, down the ravine toward the log cabin. Nighthawks were dive-bombing at insects in the open field closer to the house, catching them in mid-air with a crunch. I sat there a long time, the map of X's and the outlined body vanishing in the darkness. I never did hear Bottles scream.

12

On Saturday night I went to Three Corners with Erik and Lars. They said I could take the car if I didn't forget to come back for them. "And if you pick up Bottles, don't forget to take him home."

I had only seen Elaine's farm by moonlight. It looked different in the flat light of evening. The land stretched away from the house in narrow fields along the ridgetop, the woods crowding in on the steep slopes. The house and barn needed paint. The windmill was squeaking the way ours did when it was out of oil.

Elaine was waiting under the pine tree, wearing a wine-colored suit, her hair light against it, turned red by the sunset. She got in before I could go around to open the door for her, as though she preferred I didn't meet anyone, or that they didn't meet me. The house was dark behind her and for all I could tell she might have lived on that farm by herself, except for the dog. He came around to my side, jumped up and licked my arm.

"I see you've still got that same old dog."

"Yes."

"I left my brothers playing cards. I've got to be back there by eleven or so."

"All right."

She was sitting about four miles away from me as I drove out of the yard, her hands neatly crossed in her lap, and she looked twelve years old, on her way to a party. Somebody else's party.

"You look very nice."

"Thank you."

All she needed was a please don't muss me sign. I had a tie on, but no coat, and the way she was dressed and sitting made me feel I was wearing overalls.

I stopped the car right in the middle of the road and held out my hand. "How do you do? I'm Steve."

She laughed. "Hello, Steve. I'm Elaine."

We shook hands for a minute, then she blushed and pulled away.

"What would you like to do?"

"I don't know."

"Want to go back to the Hole in the Wall?"

She laughed. "No."

"What, then?"

"Could we just drive along the river? It's pretty there."

She showed me a shortcut down into the valley, a narrow road winding along the hillside of a dark hollow. Birds kept flying up off the gravel, their eyes shining in the car lights.

"What are they?" Elaine asked.

"Whippoorwills, I think."

The hillroad led us to a larger valley with a creek oxbowing down the middle, reflecting the sky and everything else dark. Elaine leaned back against the seat and took a deep breath. "Some people say there're still bears in this valley."

We talked about bears and wolves for a little while, my words rattling around in the car a long time after I said them.

Where the creek road ended at the Mississippi, the day was still alive, the sky a deep red close to the horizon. Several miles away, across the bright water, were tiny lights of houses in Iowa. In a little bay, close to the road, a muskrat swam out toward the main channel, leaving a long moving V on the water.

I kept waiting for the feel of a week ago to come back and I didn't know what to talk about.

"What did you do all week?"

"Haying."

"Do you help in the field?"

"I do the horse on the hayrope at the barn."

I laughed. "I still do that. Because I'm the youngest. You the youngest, too?"

"Yes. You think we'll have to do that for the rest of our lives?"

"We just might."

We drove on through the next town. A river boat with its line of barges was heading upstream, seeming to hang motionless in the red water.

Elaine was watching the boat. I reached over and tapped her on the arm. "Speak."

She laughed. "What does that mean?"

"I was imitating Bottles. It means you either exist or I'm just making you up."

"You said that before. I don't think I like it."

I put my hand on her shoulder. She sat very still, the warmth spreading into my hand and I could feel a little movement, maybe just her heart beating.

"You exist."

Then I thought of Bottles' game. Wondering if that was a small X, I pulled my hand back.

She turned toward me on the seat and didn't seem so far away. "Who is Bottles, anyway?"

"A neighbor."

"I like him," she said.

I laughed. The idea of a girl liking Bottles seemed a violation of something. "I don't think you're supposed to. You're supposed to like his brother, who's called Girls. He specializes in being liked."

"Don't you like Bottles?"

"Well, sure. I mean, I guess so. I never thought about it. He's just there."

"Not everybody is." She was sitting up straight on the seat and she sounded just like my mother.

I told her about leaving Bottles in the car all night. She leaned back and laughed. "I can just see him, walking with his book."

It was getting to be too much about Bottles.

"I'm glad you live on the ridge," I said.

"Why?"

I was thinking about Billy's sister. "Down here in the valley you'd be different. You might even already belong to somebody."

She sat up straight again. "I'm never going to belong to anybody! I'm just going to be me."

"Who's that?"

"I don't know yet. But I'll find out."

We drove about five miles without saying anything.

"What about you?" she asked. "When you finish high school next spring, what're you going to do?"

For some reason I could feel myself getting all curled up tight inside. "Hell, I don't know what I'm going to be. There's a war coming I suppose."

"I don't like wars."

I had never even thought about having a choice of liking or not liking war. It was something you just accepted. "You talk like somebody you know got killed."

"Someday somebody will."

Her face had a set, stubborn look, reminding me of Billy the night he told me he was going to be the oldest man in the world someday.

I pulled the car into a parking area. There were beer cans all over the place, and I knew if I got out I would be able to see discarded rubbers on the ground. Another X for the map, I thought.

We sat there. Her face still looked strange. I tried to decide what to do or say next. The night wasn't going the way I had imagined.

I looked out across the bottoms and realized where we were. "The soldiers wiped out Blackhawk along here someplace, killed almost all his people. Even the children. People say the soldiers went on killing them even after they tried to surrender. I think all he was trying to do was get back across the river."

Elaine was looking at me, her face in the shadows, but I could see that she was nodding. It was the first time I had thought about that battle as being war.

"They didn't catch Blackhawk himself until later. Some people say he hid for two days in a tree, with the soldiers walking all around him. After they did catch him, he tried to tell why he came across the Mississippi to get back their land. He said something like 'It was a beautiful country. I loved my towns, my cornfields, the home of my people. I fought for it!' "

Elaine had her hands up to her face and was looking out the window on her side. "I didn't know this was where it happened."

I waited, then touched her shoulder. It was shaking. I put my hand on her face and turned it toward me. Her cheeks were wet.

"Why're you crying? For Blackhawk?"

"For everything."

I gave her a little pull. She came close to me and I held her, waiting for the crying to stop. Just holding her was enough. The last red faded above the Iowa hills, but the water in the channel and sloughs was shining, reflecting the sky. Two hoot owls were calling, close to the river, seeming to answer back and forth the way I'd been told the Indians used to signal each other in the night.

I could feel Elaine moving a little each time she breathed. She wasn't crying anymore. Then she touched her cheek against my hand for a moment and pulled out of my arms.

"I'm sorry."

"I'm not. I like you, Elaine."

"I like you, Steve. Especially when you're like that."

"Like what?"

"Like just now."

I made a U-turn out of the parking place, the beer cans rattling under the wheels, and headed back down the river road. I drove slowly and it was easy to think maybe time had not passed and all those people and cornfields of Black Hawk were still there, hidden in the dark hollows or on the slopes curving up to the bluffs.

We didn't say a word to each other all the way back along the river and up the narrow creek valley. As we came onto the ridge, there was a glow on the horizon that said the moon was going to come up soon.

All at once Elaine was sitting up straight again. She began talking, words coming out right on top of each other — about the farm, which fields had oats, which had corn.

I pulled in under the pine tree. The dog didn't even get up off the walk, just thumped his tail. I put my hand on Elaine's shoulder. "Hey, what's the matter?"

"I don't know."

"Yes you do."

She bit her lip and wouldn't look at me or let me turn her face toward me. "Everything goes too fast."

"You mean us? Last time?"

She nodded. "I didn't mean to let you kiss me."

I laughed and squeezed her shoulder. "Why did you, then?"

She jerked away from my hand. I thought she was going to slap me. "Oh you're something aren't you! You think boys are so different! You think girls are just starched marshmallows or something! You think you can do anything you want with us just so you don't get us wrinkled up or pull off any buttons!"

From a long way off I could hear myself thinking, God-almighty, what the hell is going on?

She looked at me, waiting. The moon had come up and was on her face. She was prettier than ever. She took a deep breath. The front of the suit raised up and down. I watched that happening, thinking about the anatomy of it and almost forgot what we were talking about.

"There's more than just that one way to like somebody," she said.

She sat very still as if she was waiting for me to say to hell with her. I had never thought about how it might be for a girl. They were just there to be chased and if nobody chased them, how could anything ever happen?

I remembered Bottles and his damned game again. "Go back to start," I said. I got out and went around to open the door for her. "Hello Elaine. I'm Steve."

She took my hand, holding on tight, and we walked that way to the door. Her blond hair was fanned out against the wine-colored suit jacket. It was enough just looking at her.

I touched her cheek. "Next Saturday night?"

"Yes."

This time she stood and watched while I went down the walk, detouring around the sleeping dog, and got into the car and pulled out of there.

13

*T*he next day I tagged along with my brothers when they went to Gordon's Landing for a ballgame. They wouldn't let me take the car. Whichever team lost had to buy beer for everybody and Lars said they might need the car to go get it.

I walked down to the filling station and found the old man teetered back against the wall as usual. "Hey, Boy. How you making out?"

I wanted to say "I'm not," but I thought about the night before and knew I didn't want to talk about Elaine. "I'm doing all right. Where's Billy?"

"Beats the hell out of me."

"He still in Iowa?"

"He's around. Just not out of bed yet. Somebody's bed. Bastard said he'd take me fishing, too. Didn't mean a word of it."

The idea of Billy taking the old man fishing instead of the other way around seemed funny. I looked out across the river. The sun seemed brighter than usual, the sky an uninterrupted blue from one horizon of hills to the other. A cool wind was blowing in from the west, flapping the faded American flag that hung by the gaspumps every Sunday.

"By God," the old man said, "kind of day makes you feel like you're going to live forever." He turned his face into the breeze. "That wind says fall's somewhere around the corner."

I wanted to argue with him. It was a different kind of summer, or maybe a different kind of me this year and I wasn't ready for it to be heading toward an ending. "Summer's only half over."

"Don't matter. Fall's always out there waiting."

He picked up a fish pole and tackle box. "Pickup's here. How'd you like to go fishing?"

It sure wasn't my idea of how to spend Sunday afternoon in a river town, but he was standing there with the old cane pole in his hand, the pull-apart kind with brass joints, and he had a silly grin on his face. I felt maybe it was me who was ninety-some years old and he was about seven.

"I got extra stuff. You can cut a willow pole."

"All right. For a little while."

"Somebody run this Goddamn station for a change!" he yelled through the door. Nobody answered. We climbed into the pickup and headed out, leaving the place looking deserted.

He told me to drive south on the river road, then sat back on the seat, humming some tune I'd never heard before, and smiling as if we were on a big trip to Chicago. When we drove past the dam, I slowed down so we could watch a line of barges heading into the locks. A little farther on, the old man sat up straight and began nodding to himself, taking quick looks at me.

"Don't suppose you really want to go fishing, do you?"

For a minute I thought the Oldest Man in the World was going to say "Let's go find us a couple of girls."

"I don't know. Something else you wanted to do?"

"Not important. Place I'd like to look at."

"Sure. Where is it?"

He told me when to turn away from the river, onto a narrow, gravel road that wound upstream along Sand Creek. After about three miles, I saw the top branches of a big black walnut tree sticking up above all the other trees, back a ways from the road. I pulled off to the side and parked there without him saying a word.

He stared at me. For a minute I thought he might hit me.

"How'd you know?"

"Heard you talk."

He nodded. "All right. Most people don't listen. You'll find out. Someday it'll be with you just like with me. Nothing left to do but talk about how it used to be. Nobody else left to remember what it is you're talking about."

He got out of the pickup slowly, jarring down on one foot, then the other. It was the first time, since the day I met him, that I had thought of him as being old. There was a low bank along the road. I climbed up first, then reached a hand down to help him. There wasn't any fence and I led the way, crowding through the thick brush and trees, being careful not to let twigs slap back at him.

When we got into the clearing, he moved over to the walnut tree. It was four feet through and looked as if it had been there forever. Some of the leaves had fallen. The ground was yellow and brown with them and they were dry enough already to crunch under our feet. A few tiny walnuts hung in pairs on the twigs. Even if it was only about two o'clock, the place was already half in the shade because of the steep hill to the southwest.

The Oldest Man in the World looked around, nodding as he picked out each thing — a clump of lilac bushes, the leaves pale with their late summer look, the stone foundation of what must have been a house, with the bricks of two chimneys sticking up four or five feet. There were weeds and brush and two good-sized walnut trees growing out of the ruins. A few mounds and stones marked where other buildings must have been.

The old man turned and saw me watching him. "Used to be a

spring. God that water was cold. Back there behind the house, close to the hill."

He got down on his hands and knees, then turned so he was sitting, doing it all in slow motion, and leaned back against the walnut tree.

I checked on the spring. It was nothing but a little silted-in pond with moss, scraggly watercress and a few cattail reeds growing in it. A trickle of water came out of the pond and ran under the road through a metal culvert. I could hear bees working the pink flowers of wild bergamot along the hillside and the sound of wind in the trees way up on the ridge. A catbird was meowing at me. Thinking about it, I realized there always seemed to be a pair of catbirds wherever there were lilacs.

The old man's eyes were half closed and he might have been asleep except that his face kept changing. He'd nod, shake his head, smile. Once he laughed and hit his hand against his thigh.

It didn't seem I should be watching him that way, so I found a stick and began cleaning the spring, following the water back toward the hillside until I found where it bubbled up out of a crack between the layers of limestone. I scooped mud out and soon had a little pool close to the rocks. It wasn't much of a spring, but that was the way it was with a lot of them now, especially during dry years. Some people said it was because too much timber had been cut and the rain and melting snow ran off into the creeks and rivers, causing floods, instead of soaking into the soil.

After a half hour or so the water cleared and was deep enough so I could dip my hands in and bring up a handful to drink. It was cold all right. My fingers were still numb from working in it. The clean water was making little channels into the muddy water of the pond.

The sun had gone from the clearing. I looked around and found an old tin can, scooped it into the spring, the water dripping out through holes in the rusty bottom, and took it over to the old man. He had his eyes open wide, staring at where the house had been.

"Spring's still running pretty good." I held out the can.

He went on staring. It seemed that whenever I saw him I had to spend some time wondering if he was dead.

"Hey! Want some water?"

He looked at me for a minute, then back at the house. "I can shut my eyes and see smoke coming out them chimneys. I can smell lilacs on those bushes. I can see the blooms, just a little lighter colored than that girl's eyes. But I'll be Goddamned if I can remember her name."

He took a deep breath. "Guess maybe it shouldn't make that much difference about her name. I remember her all right."

I thought of the night he'd talked at the station. "What happened to her?"

"Got married to somebody. Went away. Didn't matter to me 'til she was gone. Hell, I was always losing girls back then while I was chasing a new one. Didn't want any of 'em soon as I knew I could have 'em."

The tin can was almost empty, the cold water running down my arm, and in just about a minute I expected to hear violins start playing. I went to the spring, filled the can again and pushed it into his hand.

He jumped. "What's that? What's that?"

"From the spring."

He looked at me, then at the can, took a long drink, and shook his head. "Not as cold as it used to be." He laughed. "I guess you young bucks think that's all we old ones ever say."

I smiled because he'd caught me on that one.

"I don't suppose it was running that clear to start with."

"I cleaned it out some."

He nodded. "I've done that."

He drained the can and stared at it. "You're wrong if you think that's all we ever think about, how it used to be. Hell, I wouldn't want to start it all over again, same or different. But I'm sure as hell not ready for it to end either, even if I'm not good for anything besides sitting."

"You talk pretty good," I said.

"All right. Sitting and talking. You know I had seven brothers. And I'm still here. I don't know why. Seems like I'm waiting for something. Like maybe something more important's supposed to happen to me yet. But then I been feeling like that for more'n seventy years. You suppose everybody feels that way?"

I backed away. I wanted to reach out and shake him. I wanted to yell "Damn you! What the hell is it everybody's waiting to find? Or find out? Or do? Or go to? How the hell can you live almost a hundred years and not know anything more about what it all means than I do?"

He was just like my mother. He didn't hear a word I wasn't saying.

He laughed. "I guess I remember a lot of things I'd do better to forget. Like to remember her name, though."

"You'll remember. It'll come to you sometime when you're not even thinking about it."

"I don't know," he said. "Sometimes I figure I must be getting old."

I almost laughed. But he wasn't joking. He just went right on looking at where that house used to be as though he had no idea he was the Oldest Man in the World.

I waited awhile, then brought him another drink from the spring. Waving me away when I tried to help, he got up, put the can down on the house foundation and followed me through the brush to the pickup. He didn't say a word until we got to the station, then just gathered up his fishing gear and winked. "Well, maybe they'll be biting next time."

Billy was there, teetered back in the old man's chair.

"Ball game over?" I asked.

"Yeah. Your brothers were looking for you. I said I'd take you home."

We got into the pickup.

"You have to get home right away?"

"Just so I get there for milking. Couple hours yet. Why?"

Billy laughed. "Thought we might go see something."

He drove up to the ridge, turned off on a side road, then onto an old logging trail that led back to the top of the bluffs. He kept laughing and grinning, but he wouldn't tell me anything. Finally, he pulled into the woods and parked where the brush hid the truck.

We walked toward the bluffs. I could see the dusty blue of empty space ahead, then the river far below, all the islands reaching out toward the Iowa side. Billy began moving very carefully, cutting back to the left until we hit the logging trail again. There was another truck parked there. It was the game warden's.

"I figure they don't just come up here to see the sunset," Billy whispered.

Where the woods ended, the top of the hill was covered with deep, bowed-over grass. It sloped, gently at first, then steeply down to where the rocks began. There, I knew it dropped off almost straight down several hundred feet to the valley.

The two of them were sitting, half hidden in the grass, looking out over the river. We could hear their voices but not what they were saying. He had his arm around her shoulders, her hair hanging down over it, a deep red in the late afternoon light.

Billy was still grinning. "Just give them time."

I finally realized what he was expecting. I remembered the way she had talked to me that day at Elm Springs.

"Come on, Billy. Let's get out of here."

"No. And if you make any noise, they'll see us and know we been watching."

The warden moved his arm down to her waist and pulled her toward him. She stayed that way for a minute, kissing him, then suddenly pulled away, jumped up and ran along the slope. I could hear her laughing. Her hair was floating up and down.

"Jesus!" Billy said. "I'll bet she's something."

The warden ran after her. She fell and started rolling down the slope, still laughing, arms at her sides, reminding me of how we'd done that when I was younger, always angling off because we were wider at the shoulders. It didn't happen that way with her. Hips, I thought. She's got bigger hips than boys do. I began to think about that. She rolled almost to the rocks. He followed her and pulled her up. His green shirt had dark patches of sweat.

"Look at that!" Billy said. "I'll bet they're not even married."

"Why?"

"Hell, married people don't act like that."

The two of them stayed close together longer this time, but she pulled back, let him almost catch her, and moved away again. Then she turned around and walked straight to him and began unbuttoning his shirt.

"Jesus," Billy said. "Jesus."

I gave him a pull. "Come on."

"Where you going?"

"Out of here."

"What you talking about?"

"I don't know. Come on!"

"I'm not going anywhere!"

"Yes you are."

"Why the hell for?"

"Because she was very nice to me one time."

Billy laughed. "Well, well. She was, was she? Now she's about to be nice to somebody else."

My hand had closed over a rock and in a minute I was going to hit him right in the middle of his laugh.

"Billy, I'm going back to the pickup. I'm going to blow the horn if you don't come right now."

"Sure you will." He was still watching them.

I ran into the woods to the truck and held the horn button down. Billy came running up, breathing hard. "Damn you! You got to be crazy!"

He jumped in and we roared out of there, sticks and rocks banging up under the fenders.

"Jesus, that was a dumb thing to do. That guy's big enough to kill us. He carries a gun, too!"

"He couldn't shoot us."

"Why the hell not? I'd shoot anybody that did that to me!"

"He's the game warden. There's no open season on people."

Billy laughed. "Boy, ain't she something, though?"

He drove back to the main road and turned to take me home, grinning again and saying "Jesus!" every few minutes.

"I don't think he'd approve," I said.

"The warden?"

"No. Jesus."

"Aw shut up," Billy said, but he wasn't mad at me anymore.

14

On Saturday night Elaine and I walked into Jake's Tavern in a river town called Indian Springs and the first thing I noticed was the jukebox playing "It Makes No Difference Now." I looked around and sure enough, Bottles was sitting in a booth, slumped over a beer. We went over to him.

"I figured it would be you, with that song playing."

Bottles didn't even look up. "More trouble than you think. Silly jukebox didn't even have it. Had to talk Jake into putting it on."

"Why the hell should he?"

"Symbol for our time."

"Goddamn it, Bottles! It's got nothing to do with our time! You might as well put on 'America The Beautiful' or 'Star Spangled Banner!' I can just hear 'Star Spangled Banner' going in a tavern full of drunks!"

The room was suddenly quiet. People were looking at me. A big man in bib overalls slid off a barstool and loomed over me.

"Ok, Sonny. What you got against the 'Star Spangled Banner?' "

"Well, nothing."

"Then what you mouthing off about?"

"I just think it's not the right place for it. A place like this."

"I agree with the kid!" another man yelled and started toward us.

The big man met him halfway. They began pushing at each other.

"Since when you been such a flag waver?"

"Look, pot-licker, my ancestors settled this country!"

"Hell, my ancestors been in this country longer'n yours been out of jail."

"I got relatives fought in every war this country ever had!"

"Yeah? Which side?"

The big man hauled back his fist. Jake grabbed his arm and got thrown halfway across the room. The smaller man kicked the big man in the shins. While the big man was jumping up and down, the other man circled around and made a flying tackle from behind. They both went down. The whole place rattled. A row of bottles fell off the back bar. I grabbed Elaine and went for the door. Bottles followed, still carrying his beer. Half the people in the place were fighting now.

Outside, we stopped and listened to the crashing and yelling. In a minute the town marshal's car pulled up. He jumped out and yelled, "What the hell's going on in there?"

"Maybe you should let them alone," Bottles said. "It's a very patriotic fight."

"Something about the 'Star Spangled Banner,' " I said.

"I don't believe it," the marshal said and ran inside.

The noise slowly went back to normal. In a few minutes the marshal came out leading the big man who was in handcuffs, had a bottle of whisky in both hands and was trying to drink. "That Jake's sure a nice man," he said.

Then he saw us. He pointed at me with the bottle. "There he is, Marshal! That's the bastard started the whole thing!"

"Aw, hell," the marshal said, "Jake wouldn't let him in there. He's too young."

"Damn it! He was there. Made some dispar, disparin. . . ."

"Disparaging?" Bottles said.

"Yeah, disparaging remarks about our national anthem."

The marshal looked at me. "What about it?"

"Just a minute, officer," Bottles said. He held the beer behind him and stood up very straight. "I was a witness to the entire proceedings.

There is absolutely no question that it was this party you have already taken into custody who first engaged in physical abuse."

The marshal just stared at Bottles. The big man had his mouth open, but he didn't say a word.

"Oh, for Christ sake, come on!" the marshal said. He pushed the big man into the car and drove off, red lights flashing.

"I am amazed," Bottles said, "at man's persistent inhumanity to man." He stuck his head in the door. "Hey, Jake! Is it safe to come back?"

"Sure."

Everybody was drinking again as if nothing had happened. Jake was sweeping up broken glass behind the bar and laughing so hard he could hardly stand up. He waved at us. "You three go back to the rear booth and stay out of trouble."

In a minute he brought beers for Bottles and me and a soft drink for Elaine. He sat down by Bottles, still laughing, wiping tears out of his eyes. "By God, that's the most fun we had in here since the time Fred Wilmer ducked in for a quick one just before his wedding and got his foot stuck in the spittoon."

He looked us over and shook hands with us. "I'm Jake. How'd this all get started?"

I pointed at Bottles. "He claims that record you put on is the great song of our time."

Jake shrugged. "Maybe it is."

He turned to Bottles. "Tell you what. I got a string of jukeboxes in twenty-three taverns. You convince me, I'll put it on every one. Might even turn up the volume on all those boxes so it'll follow you from one tavern to the next."

"My God!" Bottles said. "That's better than having all the springs in the country start putting out cold beer."

"Then convince me."

Bottles pointed his finger at Jake. "Song's true, that's all. Nothing makes any difference when it's over. It is better to have failed your VD test than never to have loved at all."

I looked at Elaine. She was all relaxed, watching him with her head at an angle as though they talked about VD all the time at her house.

"Hell," Bottles said. "You got people in here not twenty years old crying in their beer about the good old days. You know what they're going to do?"

Jake smiled. "I have a feeling you're going to tell me."

"They're going to spend the rest of their damn lives talking about the past and they haven't even got one."

Jake looked at me. "Well?"

I had a feeling Bottles was trying to wipe out Elaine, and Anne before her, as if they had never existed at all or maybe were just made up and used as something to be sad about when I lost them.

"Damnit, it makes a difference to me!"

"Doesn't matter," Bottles said. "Find another statue. Hit it on the foot. Hit it again. Get at its ultimate. Keep on 'til one speaks your name."

Elaine was still looking at him that way.

Jake was staring at us as if we were crazy.

"All right, Bottles!" I yelled. "What about you? How many statues you breathing life into?"

Bottles smiled. It was like watching a smile happen on the face of the Oldest Man in the World. "I'm still doing what you're doing. I'm hitting myself on the foot, yelling 'speak.' "

"Then what the hell's the difference?"

He reached out and patted me on the head. "I know whose foot I'm hitting."

Jake laughed. "By God, I don't even know what you two're talking about. But I'm going to fix it so that record'll play about twenty times."

He went to the jukebox, opened the front with a key and leaned in. We could see the stack of records and the player. Elaine laughed. "You know, I used to think there was a little miniature orchestra inside a jukebox."

The song started playing. Jake came back to the booth and looked down at us, beaming. "By God, you three are something."

Elaine was still laughing about the jukebox and I had my hand on her shoulder. Jake looked at us for quite awhile. "You two are something special. I mean, really special. You brighten this place up. It's like somebody forgot and washed the windows."

Elaine looked at me, then lowered her eyes. Her face was red.

Jake looked at Bottles. "You're something, too. I'm not even sure I like you. You're a trouble-maker of some kind. The kind of bastard that'll do anything. Likely going downhill, too. Couple years from now I could be throwing you out of here every night at closing time."

"Two years?" Bottles said. "Thank you. Maybe you don't like me because I might see who you really are."

Jake laughed. "By God, you could be right."

He brought us more drinks. "You two sure are a picture," he said, looking at Elaine and me. When he got back behind the bar, he rang a bell. "All right, everybody! Fruit basket turn-over!"

Everyone at the bar immediately got up and moved over two seats, men to the right, women to the left. They did it without protesting or asking any questions.

Jake saw us watching. "Do that all the time. Otherwise a bar's just a drinking place, not respectable. So far I take credit for fourteen marriages, three divorces and God knows how many kids."

"It Makes No Difference Now" ended and started again. Jake set up drinks for everybody, then moved along the bar, listening in on all the new conversations. A woman at one end wasn't talking to anybody. He shoved her barstool in between two men who were arguing about who had been drunkest the night before, each claiming he had.

"Here, argue over something worthwhile," Jake said.

He brought us two more beers. "Hey," he said to Bottles. "Got something for you. I'm keeping track what kind of songs people play. Happy, love successful or sad, love unsuccessful. There's a little thing-ama-bob in each jukebox registers how many times a record gets played so you know which ones to change. For a couple of months I'm leaving all the same ones on, keeping track."

"I'll bet you something," Bottles said.

"All right."

"I'll bet you figure 'It Makes No Difference' is sad, unsuccessful."

"That's right."

"It isn't. It's a happy song. The guy's admitting it's over."

Jake whacked Bottles on the shoulder. "I knew I wasn't going to like you." He went back to the bar.

Bottles spread his hands and shrugged. "God, it's hard being a prophet." He knocked over an empty beer bottle and it rolled to the floor and broke.

"Nice going, Bottles," I said. "Broken Bottles."

He slid down to pick up the pieces and disappeared.

"Hey," Elaine said, "what is his name?"

"I don't know. I don't even know if he has one."

Bottles came back into sight, a big smile on his face. "Sure, I got a name. That's broken, too. Long time ago. By streams too wide for leaping, the barefoot broken Bottles is sleeping."

Elaine reached out and touched his hand. "Hello there, Broken Bottles."

He stared at her, his face red.

I was getting angry again, and I didn't know why. I certainly wasn't jealous. How could anybody be jealous of Bottles?

He put his hand on my shoulder. He was still smiling and looked almost sober for a change. "Hey there, old disciplined, Steve. Old all-thoughts-hidden, Steve. You ever miss a younger you? Ever look back to a time you were still just you? I mean no one had pulled you off yet in a thousand directions? You ever cry 'cause you can't get all the Humpty-Dumpty pieces back together, be just you again 'stead of all shattered, forever and ever, amen?"

I felt a chill go through me. Rabbits, I thought, and I was in the back seat of the car in High Ridge.

Elaine was smiling, not seeing anything. She's up in that damn pine tree in her front yard, I thought. For a moment I wanted to be honest, wanted to say I was glad to find out somebody else felt that way. But Bottles was smiling. Elaine was smiling. Something about it made me angrier than ever.

I pushed his hand away. "I still am the real me."

Bottles bowed, tipping beer onto the table. "Forgive me." He turned to Elaine, picked up her hand and studied it. "What about you?"

She laughed. "I'm just Elaine. I don't know if that's somebody or not."

"That's somebody," I said.

Bottles still had her hand. In a minute I was going to jerk it away.

"Me, I'm somebody all mixed up," Bottles said. "Except for the part that was born old. That's a problem, too. Somebody going to ask why?"

"Why?" Elaine said.

"Tell you why. Because that part knows exactly what's going to happen, but other part can't do anything to change it."

I realized there was somebody standing at the booth. It was the going-steady couple. I had to work at it to remember their names were Willy and Marge.

"You got a car?" Willy asked.

"Yeah."

"Can we get a ride when you go? We're over at the dance." The girl was smiling to herself.

"Sure." I watched them go, shaking my head.

"How come they make you mad?" Bottles asked.

I wanted to say something about everything standing still forever like a horse going around and around in endless circles on a sorghum cane grinder.

"They don't!" I said.

Bottles let go of Elaine's hand, poured beer into his glass, partly missing, and raised it in a toast. "Goodbye again, Steve."

"I wish you'd stop saying that."

"Me this time. Heading West, the Great Plains. Going to follow the wheat harvest. Want to know why?"

He lifted his glass again. "I'm looking in distance for all the things I've lost somewhere in time."

I laughed. "What a voice that beer's got in it."

Elaine was looking at Bottles as though she had never seen him before. "Maybe you never found any of those things in the first place."

He blinked at her. "Yeah, that's what I mean."

I picked up his beer and took a drink. "Then why didn't you say so?"

"I didn't know that's what I meant when I said it."

Elaine laughed.

I drained the glass and banged it down in front of him. "You need another beer."

I took hold of Elaine's arm and hauled her out of the booth. "Come on!"

We headed for the door.

"Hey, you two," Jake called. "You come back. You sure do brighten this place up." He was beaming at us, a short, roly-poly man with a round face, and back beyond him I could see Bottles watching, slumped down in the booth, his hair mussed up and he all at once looked a lot younger.

We went across the street to the dance hall. Elaine would answer when I spoke. She would smile when I looked at her. But she wasn't there. I pulled her tight against me while we danced. She was only warm on the outside. The more I tried to talk, the farther away she went.

Pretty soon I gave up. I tried to signal to the going-steady couple, but they were dancing, staring off into space and couldn't see me. I had to chase them down and tap them on the shoulder to wake them up.

We started home, Elaine sitting very still, clear over by the door. In the rear-view mirror I could see Willy and Marge. He was draped all over her and she was looking out the window.

The night was still warm. When we came up onto the ridge, the moon was hanging very big on the horizon. There was the feel of dew in the air and the smell of wetted dust. Fog covered part of the valley below us, the river reflecting the moonlight.

I didn't try to talk to Elaine. The night might have ended that way if it hadn't been for the cows.

Just before we got to Marge's house, we came around a sharp curve on the state highway and the cows were all over the road. I slammed on the brakes. Willy and Marge flopped against the back of the front seat. A big black and white Holstein was looking at us over the radiator ornament, chewing her cud. I blew the horn. She galloped off, along with about a dozen others, hoofs clattering on the blacktop.

I left the lights on and ran after them, looking for a gate to chase them through. The car door slammed and Elaine was running beside me. We had the cows headed toward the farmhouse when about twenty more came galloping from the opposite direction. They met head on and began going in circles, bawling.

I saw a flash of white. A man was chasing them, yelling. Farther back, somebody smaller was running after him, calling. "Pa! Pa! Ma says you got to put this on!"

Some of the cows got past us. I heard tires squeal. There were more headlights now. A car pulled in beside mine. A whole bunch of boys jumped out and began running and yelling.

"Yippi! Roundup time!"

"Where are we chasing them?"

"Who cares?"

"Where the hell's the gate?"

Elaine was still beside me.

A cow came by with a dog hanging onto its tail, the dog trying to hold back, its claws scraping along the road. One of the boys from the other car saw the dog. He grabbed the tail of the cow ahead of him, trying to do the same thing. The cow headed for the side of the road. The boy went sliding into the ditch. It had cattails sticking up out of it. I could hear the splash as the boy and cow went in. The boy came crawling out, covered with mud.

Another boy chased a cow to the opposite side. Wire creaked. "Damn!" he yelled. "Damn! Damn!"

Some of the cows stopped running and began eating grass along the edge of the blacktop. The man was pushing at one and whacking her on the back with his hands. She went right on eating. He twisted her tail. She bawled and ran. I tried to head her off and went past the boy who was holding something out toward the man. "Here, Pa. Ma says. . . ."

I couldn't see Elaine anywhere.

A cow jumped the ditch. Wire creaked as she hit the fence. There was a sharp, ringing ping, then another, another and another. Staples were pulling out of the fence posts.

The young boy came by me again. The man was chasing him this time, yelling. "The gate! The gate! I told you and told you! Shut the gate!"

He caught up and began flailing at the boy. The boy had his arms wrapped around his head and was ducking pretty good. "The gate! You said you closed the gate!"

The man's arms seemed to get tired. He stood there saying, "The gate! The gate!"

The boy took his hands down from his head. "If you're all through doing that, maybe we better get the cows in." He held out what he was carrying. It was a long nightgown. "Ma says for you to put this on."

The man looked down. He wasn't wearing anything but a shirt. He put one hand in front of his crotch. With the other he grabbed the nightgown, then went running off again.

The boy saw me watching. He laughed. "He's all right. He always gets a little crazy when the cows get out."

My God, it's a pity Bottles is missing all this, I thought.

There was a lot of yelling back toward the cars. I heard a batch of cows galloping toward me. Somebody was riding one of them. It started bucking. The boy went rolling into the ditch. He got up, stumbled, fell down again. When he finally got up, I saw it was Willy. I'd never heard him laughing before.

I tried to stop the cow that had bucked him off, and I ran full speed into Elaine. We both went over backward. The cow stopped and began licking Elaine on the face. She was laughing so hard she couldn't get up.

The dog came by and grabbed the cow's tail. The cow kicked the dog and sent it rolling along the road, yelping. Other cars had stopped, the light blinding the cows so that they were running into everything. All the yelling moved farther up the road. The man came by, holding the nightgown in one hand, the other trying to hide his crotch. The cows were finally running through a gate into the field. The man stood gasping, saying, "Thank. Thank. Thank."

I reached out my hand to Elaine. She was still laughing.

"Hello, Elaine."

"Hello, Steve."

I pulled her up and we walked to the car, holding hands. Marge was still in the back seat, looking out the window and nodding a little as though she saw things like this all the time.

Willy came running up. He was grinning and had a big rip in his shirt. "By God! We got to do this more often." He climbed in, hauled Marge over to him and put his arms around her.

"Ugh, you're all sweaty."

I watched them in the mirror, waiting for Willy to apologize. He just laughed, held her where she was and said, "Aw, shut up, Marge." Suddenly I liked him better.

When we got to Marge's house, Willy came around to my side and whispered. "See you a minute?"

I got out and followed to the front of the car. "You mind waiting? Got a feeling I might get there tonight."

"OK," I said.

He ran after Marge toward the dark house.

Elaine was out of the car, standing in the driveway looking at the sky, her arms stretched overhead as though she might try to pull the moon right down on top of us. A dog came up behind her and touched its nose against her bare leg. She jumped, then saw what it was and leaned down, burying her face in the fur, hugging the dog to her.

A door squeaked, but no lights came on in the house. I looked at my watch. I couldn't believe it was only a little after midnight because it seemed about three weeks ago that Elaine and I had walked into Jake's place. The air was still warm and soft, with no hint of coolness. I could smell the sweetness of corn and knew that if I was in the field I might be able to hear the slight creaking and popping noises of the growing stalks.

I smelled fresh cut hay, too, and saw where it was raked into curving windrows in a field the other side of a little ravine. Elaine was still hugging the dog, but she was looking at me. I started toward her. Something had to happen. She laughed and ran, down across the ravine toward the hayfield, looking back at me some of the time, her hair coming over her shoulders, and it seemed I had seen her that way a thousand times.

I followed her, running fast along the narrow path in the ravine and into the hayfield. I was gaining on her and wanted to catch up and pull her down. She stopped and turned to me, full into the moonlight. She opened her arms wide. I ran into them, swinging her clear off the ground and we whirled, the moon going around and around in a white streak.

Elaine pulled away. I was dizzy and fell, got up and fell again, my feet tangled in the hay. Elaine walked in a circle around me, laughing. I didn't get up, just watched her, afraid to catch up with her again. She kept walking around me, somebody I didn't even know. Somebody I might never get to the end of. I remembered Bottles saying how lonely it was with a girl. This was some other kind of loneliness.

I turned onto my back, looking at the stars. I hadn't done that much lately. The ones I knew were familiar and distant as ever. I began to feel smaller and my hands held onto the hay stubbles because I was about to vanish into nothing.

Elaine's steps came toward me. I could hear her quick breathing. She knelt beside me, hair swinging. I reached for her. She put her hands against my shoulders and held me still.

"Nobody's going to pull me off in a thousand directions!"

I had never heard her voice sound that way before.

"I'm never going to change! Never going to be old and not feel like this!"

She snuggled close to me. I moved my hands toward her. She held them. We lay side by side on our backs, cheeks touching. The moon was in just one place again. I was afraid to move or say a word. An owl began hooting far down the ravine and the crickets started again in the hayfield.

We stayed there until Willy whistled. Then I pulled her up and we walked, not saying anything, not even touching, back across the ravine to the car.

Willy came up close to me and whispered. "Almost. Next time for sure."

I took Elaine home ahead of Willy because there was nothing else that needed to be said or done with the night. At her door, I didn't even put my arms around her, just took her face in both my hands and kissed her gently for a long time.

15

After dropping Willy off, I turned onto an old hillroad leading down to a valley I had to cross on the way home. It was only one car wide, very steep, and at the bottom there was a sharp turn just before the narrow bridge crossing the dry ditch. I drove fast, knowing I wasn't likely to meet anybody. Birds flew up ahead of me, eyes shining as they wheeled away from the lights into the woods. There were flashes of changing colors from the sides, white sweet clover, brown-eyed Susans and purple bergamot, all of them with a brown covering from the road dust. On the first sharp turn I swung too wide. I could hear the flower heads ringing against the front bumper, then loose gravel pinging on the inside of the fenders as I pulled back to the center.

A little cooler air was coming up the narrow hollow, filled with the dust, dew and flower smells of the night. It reminded me of the hayfield and I drove faster. The trees leaned into the road, meeting overhead, making a dark tunnel with no moonlight coming through.

I could see the final curve up ahead. I sat up straight on the seat, gripping hard on the wheel. I braked a little just before the curve, then went into it. Loose gravel was banked up on the outside. I could see the shine of the bridge, gravel all the way across it. I slammed down the accelerator, remembering suddenly that Dad still called it a "footfeed," came sideways out of the turn and went all the way across the bridge that way, the gravel ringing on the metal rail.

The car went on sliding. I tried to pull it back, braking a little. The car hopped on the gravel and slid to a stop with both back wheels in the ditch, the car crossways on the road. I didn't even care. It was the best slide I'd ever done.

The dust was settling, thick beams of it picked out by the headlights that were shining up at the hillside across the hollow. I shut off the engine and lights. The night sounds started again, katydids rasping, the whippoorwills, and a fox barking up on the ridge.

When I got out, something moved near the bridge. "Having a little trouble?" a quiet voice said.

He moved closer. It was Harvey Shields who lived on a farm about a quarter of a mile away in the main creek valley. I had helped fill silo there once, the corn half smartweeds in the wet bottom fields. I remembered his mother, a short, heavy, bent-over woman who complained about how long it was taking to get the silo full.

He came up close and peered at me. "You, is it? I figured it might be. Tell you what, get in and try her."

I rocked the car back and forth a few times, with him pushing. It came right out and I pulled into the middle of the road and got out to check for dents.

"Looks all right," he said. "I guess nobody will ever know it happened."

He held out a small liquor bottle. "Like a little of my sleeping medicine?"

"No thanks."

He sat down on the running board. "Been out chasing girls?"
"Sure."

He watched me, waiting. "In a hayfield," I said.

He took a long drink and started nodding. "Had me a girl like that once. My mother put a stop to it. That girl moved away, up to this little town in Minnesota. Could be dead by now. Leastwise, she'd likely be married."

I thought of the older women who came alone to places like Jake's and the Hole in the Wall. "There's others around."

"Hell, first I'd have to get my mother's permission. She's mean enough to up and die just to spite me."

He pushed the bottle into my hand. "You got a good mother, Boy. I always liked your mother. Do you know the year your folks moved in up there, I can remember just how she looked first time I saw her at the school picnic. Must have been about the time the war ended, 1918 or 1919 maybe. I remember her looking at all those people with those big eyes of hers. I guess she was just about the prettiest girl I ever saw."

Girl? I thought. Girl?

He took the bottle back, not noticing I hadn't had any, finished it and threw it over the fence. It smashed in the rocks, the sound echoing off the hillside. The katydids stopped for a minute.

"Your dad's a lucky man. And what the hell have I got? A farm with a new crop of rocks on the hillside every year, mud getting deeper in the bottoms. I got that and you know what else? I got a bald head and a fat mother."

I thought of the Oldest Man in the World at the big walnut tree. It was the same all over again, only worse because Harvey Shields couldn't be more than forty years old. I stared into the darkness wondering how many people were out there wandering around, looking for something they had lost.

"Down that road, a quarter of a mile, there's the house I was born in. Inside that house there's an old woman who right this minute is snoring so loud I had to walk this far to get out of reach of it."

He leaned over to look at me and took hold of my arm. "You catch that girl in the hayfield?"

"Yes, but. . . ."

His hand tightened and he waited.

"I caught her. I guess you could say we caught each other."

He let go of my arm. "Yeah. Probably dead by now. She was sure a nice girl. Hair halfway down her back, always braided up someway. Eyes the color of those little wild aster flowers that bloom about the time school starts."

He got up and leaned against the side of the car. "You suppose that snoring's stopped yet? You know, I hear you go by here sometimes at night. Did you know that? Always wonder where you been."

"I have to be getting home."

He grabbed my arm again. "Look, would you do something?"

My God, I thought, a message for my mother?

"If I ever had a son, I'd want him like you. Want him to chase girls in a hayfield. Even get a girl in trouble or kill himself skidding across bridges instead of spending his whole Goddamned life being twelve years old, taking care of his mother."

He was staring toward the house again.

"What did you want me to do?"

"I want you to take me up to the top of this Goddamned hill. I want you to give me a ride down the Goddamned hill and go sliding sideways across the Goddamned bridge!"

He was hurting my arm, his face looking young or maybe just crazy.

"Sure," I said.

We got in. I turned the car around, drove to the top of the hill, turned around again and headed down. We picked up speed, the exhaust loud, backfiring every time I let up on the gas. He sat straight, holding onto the seat with both hands. He didn't seem to be breathing.

We came into the turn just before the bridge. I gunned it, swinging the wheel. We slid across the bridge, gravel ringing. I hauled the car back straight and stopped. It had been a good one. I had never hit the rail with that much gravel before.

"My God!" he said. "My the living God!"

He got out, very carefully closed the door, patted the car a couple times and walked down the road toward the house.

For the next week, we were haying from the minute the dew was off until close to sunset, each day just like the last, hot, dusty, endless. When Saturday night came, I felt I'd been locked away on the farm for years. Erik went to sleep at the supper table and said he was going to bed right after chores and not get up until Monday morning. Lars told me he was going to Gordon's Landing if I wanted to ride along. Suddenly I wasn't tired anymore.

"I got a poker game lined up," Lars said as we drove right on through Three Corners, straight into the red sky. "You can have the car and pick me up later."

All at once the night was filled with a million possibilities. I would come driving up, find only Elaine at home and she'd say, "Come on in, Steve." Or we'd go to the car. I'd open the door for her. She would swing the front seat forward and crawl into the back just like the girl at High Ridge.

"How much later?"

"All depends on how the game's going."

I knew where he would be playing — in the back room of the tavern. Most of the players would be older and there was something grown up and mysterious about it.

"How much do you play for?"

"Twenty-five cent limit, three raises. You can still make or lose twenty, thirty bucks."

"You got that kind of money?"

"No, that's why I don't know how much later."

He laughed, sounding all excited. "You going looking for a girl?"

"Sure."

"Same one as the night of the steamboat?"

"That didn't work out. A different one."

I was driving. I could feel him looking at me and thinking.

"All right," I said. "What?"

He laughed. "I was just wondering about the three of us. Erik's home in bed probably dreaming about radio tubes and car pistons. I'm heading for a poker game. You're off to pick up some girl the rest of us have never seen."

"What about it?"

"I don't know. Just seems funny. I never thought about it before. I guess I always figured three brothers would all be just the same. Hell, we don't even know anything about each other."

We were heading down into the darker valley now and I turned on the headlights. Lars had never talked that way before. I felt shy all at once, not sure I wanted him knowing any more about me, especially how I seemed to be thinking of girls all the time. But I still wondered about him.

"Well how come you guys never go out with girls?"

"I don't know. Just never got in the habit, I guess. Seems like a waste of time with all the other things around to do."

That didn't make any sense to me. We drove on down the hill, not speaking. After he had started talking that way, I felt we should be saying something to each other, so I told him about Harvey Shields and what had happened at the bridge.

He listened and just said, "I'll be damned."

I dropped him off at the tavern.

"Come by in an hour or so and I'll know how it's going," he said.

I sat in the car a minute, looking over at the filling station. I didn't see Billy, but the Oldest Man in the World was teetered back in his chair with the usual bunch of men around. Then I drove up-river because Elaine would be waiting. At least I hoped she would. Last Saturday night had ended in such a daze I didn't even remember if I had talked about when I would see her.

She ran out to meet me when I drove in, wearing the same white dress she'd had on that first night at the Hole in the Wall.

"Hey, do we have a date?"

She laughed. "You mean you couldn't remember either?"

She got in and slid over close to me. "I'm glad you came."

"What do you want to do?"

"I don't know," she said. "What do you?"

The house was all dark, as though no one else was there. What I wanted to do was pull her out of the car and go inside. I leaned over and kissed her, keeping both hands gripped tightly on the wheel.

"First I have to check with my brother to see how long I can keep the car."

I drove toward Gordon's Landing.

"Hey, you've got older brothers. Do they go out with girls?"

"No. They're too busy drinking all the beer in the world."

"Neither do mine. I guess we're different."

"I don't know. I'm still 'kid sister.' I never know what they're thinking."

"Lars was talking about that tonight."

She smiled. "As somebody once said, 'Nobody knows anything about anybody.' "

"Who said that, Bottles?"

"You did. At the Hole in the Wall that night."

I couldn't remember. "It must have been the beer talking."

Elaine had one of those off-by-herself expressions, reminding me of how Mom looked sometimes, and I couldn't think of anything to say.

At the tavern I opened the door to the back room. The smoke came out at me and the smell of beer and whisky. The six of them around the table all had their faces locked up tight. Everybody was looking at Lars. He was leaning back, cards cupped in both hands close to his face. He slid them apart just enough so he could see. Then he put them facedown in a neat book, pushed some coins into the pot and in a flat voice said, "I'll just have to see that and raise a quarter."

Everybody else stayed, their coins clinking into the pile. There were dollar bills in the pot, too.

Lars flipped over his cards and one by one fanned them out.

"Lucky bastard," one of the men said. The others tossed their cards in, facedown.

Very slowly Lars reached out both hands, cupped them around the money and pulled it to him.

The whole scene was totally familiar. It took me awhile to remember I had seen it in a western movie. Lars began stacking the coins, smoothing out the dollar bills. Then he saw me at the door.

"Deal me out this hand," he said and followed me outside.

He looked at the car. "Somebody with you?"

"Yeah."

"Going to introduce me?"

"If you want."

We walked over. "Elaine, this is my brother, Lars."

"Hi," she said.

"Hi." He stood there nodding, and I wanted to say "What you need to do is see another movie, one where some man from up in the hills comes down to the valley and talks with a girl for the first time."

He took my arm and walked me back toward the tavern. "Looks like a good night in there. It'll be awhile. Midnight or after."

He looked back at the car. "Pretty girl." He winked. "Take good care of her. The car, too." He tucked a couple of dollar bills into my shirt pocket and went inside.

I got in the car and roared out of there. Elaine looked at me several times. "What's the matter?"

"Nothing."

"Something about him?"

"Yeah."

She touched my arm.

"Aw hell, Elaine. What's he going to find sitting in there with a bunch of men afraid to smile because it might mean they got an ace? You know something? Ten years from now it'll be just the same as tonight. He'll still be sitting there and if he meets somebody like you all he'll be able to do is say 'Hi,' then stand there shifting his feet back and forth."

"Why does that make you so mad?"

"Not knowing what makes me so mad is what makes me so mad!"

I headed up the hill, still driving fast, wanting to get out of the valley. An hour ago I'd been coming down that hill half choked up because Lars and I seemed to be getting to know each other a little for the first time. Now he was in that back room again, killing time, like Billy or Bottles or me, while we each waited to be the oldest man in the world.

At the top of the hill I noticed the road Billy and I had turned into when he took me to see the warden and his wife. I drove on past and could see the lights of Gordon's Landing way down below us.

"There's a saying that the Devil spends extra time in a river town. Did you ever hear that?"

"No." Her hand tightened on my arm. "Where are we going?"

"I don't know. Hey, you ever been to that park where you can look down and see the Wisconsin and Mississippi Rivers meet? You been there?"

She shook her head.

"Want to go?"

She clapped her hands. "I know! A picnic! Could we have a picnic?"

"Hot dogs," I said.

"And marshmallows!"

The lights were still on in a little crossroads store. We stopped there and raced each other in, laughing. Country music was playing on the radio. A woman in bib overalls was sitting behind the counter, a big yellow cat in her arms. We both began talking at once.

"Wait, wait, wait."

She turned off the radio. "Now, you're going on a picnic. You just now thought of it. You don't have anything with you."

"Right."

We stood in front of her, holding hands. She put the cat down and it began rubbing against our legs. I could smell spices and smoked meat.

The woman touched Elaine's sleeve, feeling the material. "My, my, aren't you a pretty one." The cat jumped back onto the counter and she pushed it off. "All right," she said. "What do you need?"

"Half dozen hot dogs."

"Half dozen buns."

"Some orange pop."

"And marshmallows," Elaine said.

The woman was smiling, reminding me of the way Jake kept looking at us. We followed her around the store as she gathered up the things and put them into a bag. Back at the counter, she thought for a minute. "Napkins," she said. She broke open a package and put some in, then looked into the bag again. "Ketchup and mustard," she said. "No good without that. Wait a minute."

She went through a door at the far end of the store, the cat following her. In a minute she came out, holding up a little jar. "There. I mixed some together."

Elaine ran to her and whispered something. The woman gave her a hug, pulled something else off the shelf and put it in the bag. "Of course. You have to have dessert."

"We've already got marshmallows."

The woman came back to the counter and patted me on the head. "Now just never you mind." She handed the bag to Elaine. "You better carry it."

"How much is it?" I asked.

She spread her hands and laughed. "My goodness, I don't know. How much should a picnic cost? How about fifty cents?"

I pulled one of the dollar bills out of my shirt pocket. "How about a dollar?"

She started to push it back at me.

"We could figure it's my brother who's paying," I said. "He gave me some of his poker winnings."

"All right."

When we got in the car, she was standing in the door watching us. I got out again, went back and stuck out my hand. With her in bib overalls that seemed the right thing to do. "Thank you very much."

She shook my hand, giving it a good squeeze. I turned away quickly because she looked about ready to cry.

Elaine was holding the paper bag in her lap, looking at me across it and laughing as I pulled onto the road.

"What are you laughing at?"

"You. When you went back, I was sure you were going to ask her to come along."

"Didn't think of it or I would have."

When we drove into the park, the car lights began finding the bright, bright blue of flowers along the edge of the narrow road. I knew they could only be asters and I couldn't believe the summer was that close to being over.

I parked by a sign with an arrow and the words "Green Cloud Hill."

"That way," Elaine said.

"First we have to see the rivers."

She insisted on carrying the bag of food. I took her other hand and we ran along the twisting top of a long serpent-shaped Indian mound, fallen leaves rattling under our feet. Katydids were rasping in the woods on our left. A new coolness came up over the edge of the bluff as we got close. Then far below there was the shine of water, bright against the black shapes of the shores and islands, low fog rising from the place where the two rivers met. A little sunset red hung close above the Iowa side, shading into deep blue higher up, with stars shining.

A riverboat, still out of sight to the south, was reaching far ahead with a searchlight, finding its way upstream. I could hear Elaine's quick breathing. The breeze was swinging her hair and she lifted it with her hand and held it up off her neck.

"It's beautiful," she said.

I went on looking at her. "Yes."

I wanted to pull her into my arms and knew that would turn it into something else. I wanted to say something, but there were tears in my eyes and I didn't trust my voice.

Maybe she knew. She looked at me, gave my hand a squeeze and let go.

We went on toward Green Cloud Hill, along a dark, tree-covered trail, until we came to a little meadow where the sky was open above us. Bent way over so we could see, we searched for twigs and sticks at the edge of the woods. Elaine was a white shape, disappearing and appearing as she walked among the trees.

"You look like a ghost!"

She vanished. In a minute I heard footsteps running up behind me. I turned. The white was coming at me. I knew, but the little shiver went through me anyway because all my life there had been something watching me and waiting in the darkness.

"Boo!" she yelled, laughing.

I started the fire in a circle of rocks at the edge of the clearing. The sudden flames blinded us, lighting up the oak leaves above, making everything very dark out beyond the reach of the fire. With my pocket knife, I cut two long, slim sticks from fallen branches. I handed one to her and whipped the air with mine.

"If it was a picnic with my brothers, back a few years, we'd have to have a sword fight before letting them be just hotdog sticks."

Elaine was on the other side of the fire. "On guard!" I yelled and fenced with the flames.

She laughed. "That's how I like you. All interested in things that way."

"Instead of just you."

She was blushing. "Yes."

"Hey, you're still afraid of me."

"Of us."

I put the stick under my arm and stuck my hands in my pockets. "There, you're safe."

In a few minutes the smell of the roasting hot dogs filled the night. They had a coating of ashes and were dripping, the drops of fat sputtering, flaring up, pushing the darkness back. Elaine was kneeling close to the fire, her face, hair and dress all turned to orange.

We finished the hot dogs and roasted marshmallows on the same sticks.

"Ready for dessert?" Elaine asked. She took a little cake out of the bag and tore the cellophane off.

"I couldn't eat another bite."

"Yes you can. It's my birthday."

"Aw, hell. I forgot all about it. I'm sorry, Elaine."

"That's all right."

"No, it isn't. If I could say when it was even before you told me, how could I forget?"

I knew all right. I could almost see Bottles standing just outside the rim of firelight, saying "Ultimates don't have birthdays."

She put the cake down on a rock. I tore out seventeen paper matches, stuck them into the cake and lighted them.

"Make a wish."

She looked at me, then blew them all out in one breath.

I touched her on the shoulder with an unsticky part of my hotdog stick. "I dub thee seventeen."

She borrowed my knife, cut the cake and handed me a piece. "Now, in our family the birthday person has to finish their cake without saying a word."

She took a bite.

"In our family, we used to get a spank for each year," I said. "Then one to grow on."

She shook her head.

"That's eighteen spanks. Maybe I should do that."

She was laughing and made a "hunh-uh" noise.

"Isn't that a word?"

"Hunh-uh."

She was sitting down now, shoes off, dress pulled up a little into her lap, her legs long and smooth, and she was somebody I'd been dreaming about being on a picnic with for what seemed like half of my life.

She put the last of the piece of cake in her mouth. "There."

"What did you wish?"

"I can't tell you. Later, maybe."

"Hey, now we're both seventeen."

"Yes. Do I look older?"

"You look like Elaine."

She nodded. "When's your birthday?"

"May."

"Then we'll have to have a first picnic of the year for yours."

She crumbled the rest of the cake and scattered it on the stones. For quite awhile we both sat staring into the dying fire, its column of blue smoke and sparks going up into the oaks. There were noises in the woods, acorns dropping, an owl hooting, the katydids, and something else — a slight rustling sound as though little night creatures were playing in the fallen leaves. Or maybe not. Maybe some left over life from the Indian days, something not yet quite lost in what had come to take the place of all that.

When the fire was out, we went back to the car, bringing the smell of smoke inside with us. An acorn fell on the roof and took a long time rolling off. Elaine moved, her clothes rustling. I pulled her over to me and kissed her, rougher than I intended and couldn't stop. She jerked away, my hand brushing across the front of her dress. I heard her take a quick breath. She moved close to the door and stayed there.

We started home. After a while she began asking about the Indian mounds. I told her what I knew and it was all a nice, safe history lesson.

At her door, I put my hands behind my back and kissed her. "Hey," I said. "You taste like mustard and ketchup."

She laughed and put her head against me. We stood that way for a long time, not moving, and it was all right again.

I fell asleep in the car while I waited for Lars to finish his game and didn't wake up until we were home.

"Did you win?"

"Sure."

"How much?"

"That, little brother, is something you never tell."

I moved up close so I could see him in the moonlight. He had on his western movie face again, only this time it was worse. He looked smug, too. I wanted to yell at him. I wanted to kick him in the shins and wipe that look off his face. He just went on pulling bills from his pockets and smoothing them out and it wasn't any use. He didn't even know I was there.

I ran to the house. After changing clothes, I grabbed a blanket, crawled out through the window and ran across the garden into the alfalfa field. There was a coolness close to the ground when I spread out the blanket and lay down on my back. I could feel the dew coming through my clothes, my mind falling toward the stars and Elaine could not or would not go with me.

The wetness on my face wasn't all dew. The end of the evening, when we had been closer together again, was gone. I was back at the picnic. She was jerking away from me, her face saying there was something wrong with me for wanting what I was wanting.

"I've got two Elaines," I said.

One of them was sitting in the firelight and all I wanted to do was be there with her. The other Elaine was warm and moving under my hands and I wanted to do a lot more.

I sat up. My shadow, very definite in the bright moonlight, sat up with me. My God, are there two of everybody? I thought. Two of me? Two of Elaine? Two of Lars?

I had a sudden image of Bottles thinking about that, eyes very round, his head shaking. "No, I think there would be rather more than just two of everybody. You see, there's who you think. . . ."

Bottles kept talking. Elaine kept pulling away. Lars kept wearing his movie face. I never did go to sleep. When first light came, I was still sitting up, wrapped in the blanket, shivering, hearing the horned larks singing as they flew up almost out of sight and then came falling out of the sky.

After breakfast, Mom stopped me in the kitchen. "Bottles came by last night." She held out a box. "He left this for you."

It was a fly-fishing outfit. I had never seen one except in the catalogs. I turned the butt section of the split bamboo rod around in my hand, feeling the smooth, soft cork, trying to figure out what was going on.

"He said to tell you goodbye."

"He's already gone out West?"

"Yes. Then he says he's coming back and go to college."

That was harder to believe than the fly rod. There was a note in the box:

"Dear Steve,

It's the season for everything changing. We sold the car to a man who is selling it to a man in Milwaukee. Tools is part of the deal. He goes along to keep it running. So he'll be all right. Girls is still someplace in Iowa, I guess. We know what he'll be doing. He'll be all right anyplace. I'm going to see if college is maybe some kind of an ultimate, too. Or instead of. There's a brewery in the same town, so I'll be all right. That leaves our old man. Maybe you could roll a tire down the hill for him sometime when he wants to target shoot. I got the fishing outfit one time I read a book by Thoreau. He seemed to like fishing. But maybe it was just so nobody would laugh when he watched birds.

Bottles"

I read it about three times, then handed it to Mom, deciding the word "ultimate" wasn't going to mean anything to her.

"I don't believe it," I said.

"What?"

"Any of it. Mostly the college part."

"I do. I told him I was glad."

"That's just to get him away from me! So maybe in college he'll learn to get his hair cut more often!"

She looked at me, the way she might have when I was six years old. "I like your fishing outfit."

That only made me angrier. "I don't understand half of what goes on in this damn world!" I waited for her to pounce on me for saying "damn."

She just smiled. "I don't think that's true. I don't think anyone understands as much as half. What you mean is you don't understand a fiftieth, or maybe a hundredth."

I had a feeling she wasn't going to let go, no matter what I said. It was what Dad called a taffy-pulling conversation with everything getting stickier and stickier.

She went into the dining room with a stack of plates and came out in a minute using her apron to wipe dust off a green leather-bound book. "Here. Try reading some Thoreau yourself. Maybe you'll find out a little more about what's going on."

"What do you know about Thoreau?"

"Don't forget I went to college myself."

I knew that all right, but I didn't remember it very often. At the moment it seemed as strange as the idea of Bottles going.

I went outside, climbed up into a tree and began reading *Walden*. The first part reminded me of all the time I had spent by myself in the woods and along the creek. That didn't seem to have anything to do with now. Pretty soon I skipped over to the back and found a part that reminded me of the last time I had looked for Anne at Elm Springs. "I left the woods for as good a reason as I went there. Perhaps it seemed to me that I had several more lives to live, and could not spare any more time for that one."

That made sense to me all right.

There was another part that I remembered best of all — "It is not worthwhile to go round the world to count the cats in Zanzibar." The words kept going on and on inside me that afternoon when I went down to the creek to try fly-fishing.

There were four young boys fishing from the bank with willow poles and worms. They laughed their heads off while I thrashed the line back and forth, catching bull thistles, nettles, fence wires and every low-hanging willow limb in sight.

For the rest of the week I ran to the creek every day right after chores, going on downstream where the willows hid me while I taught myself to fly-fish. It was a funny time, as though I had turned around and gone back to my last year in grade school and was still wandering home by myself each night. Every time I thought about Elaine, I pushed her right out of my mind again.

There was an old orchard above the creek. After eating a few hundred apples, managing to avoid most of the worms, I began to get the fly landing where I wanted it about once every ten tries. I caught lots of chubs, which made grunting noises when I took them off the hook, but the trout never appeared.

On Friday afternoon I sat for a long time on the hillside above the creek. Maybe the book had done that to me, made me more willing just to watch everything. There was a great grove of white pines a little way up the hill and an old log cabin, all fallen in except for the door. That was made of three-inch thick planks, with the heavy door frame still around it. Something about it made me want to walk up to it and knock, then run around to the other side and let myself in, but I had always been afraid to do that.

The day changed as I watched. The sun went down over the hills and I knew I should be going home. A big flock of blackbirds rattled the drying corn next to the creek. A long way off, I could hear a steel-wheeled wagon on a gravel road, probably coming home from silo filling which was early because of the dry weather. The wind started up, making just a little sound in the tops of the tallest pines. Every few minutes a killdeer went screaming up from along the creek. In one of the dark ravines, where night came early, a lone whippoorwill was calling, pretending summer wasn't almost over.

I listened, not letting myself think anything, but suddenly my heart was pounding the way it used to do when I knew something was waiting just out of sight in the darkness. My back was toward the old cabin. I was sure someone was at the door, watching me. I thought of the darkhaired girl who kept running away from me in the dream and I had a crazy feeling she might be someone who had lived there. Then I knew who it was. It was Anne. She was waiting for something that was still supposed to happen. It hadn't ended after all that day I yelled goodbye to the empty shack.

The whippoorwill stopped in the middle of a call. A long way off I could hear a voice. I whirled. There was nothing, not even a sense of something slipping away just as I turned. I still wasn't sure and I ran over and looked behind the old door, feeling foolish when no one was there. Below the cabin, the creek had become a ribbon of light, reflecting the pink sky. The water stirred where a riffle ran down into a deep pool. It was a trout, taking insects off the top of the water.

I got the rod all ready, my hands shaking, and crept down to the creek. Watercress pulled at my ankles. I could feel cold water pouring into my shoes and the smell of mint came up.

The trout rolled again, about thirty feet away. I started the line going back and forth, behind me and ahead of me in rolling loops, then let it fall. The fly went too high, the line wrapping around a twig. I pulled gently. The leader unwound itself. The fly dropped. I wasn't sure it ever touched the water. There was a flash. The rod almost jerked out of my hands. The line ran back and forth, cutting the water with a sharp whine. I managed to keep the line tight, even when the trout ran toward me. It stayed deep and I couldn't see it. My arm was getting tired. The fish made a long run toward the lower end of the pool, coming close to the top now, flashing gold and red. The current was with it and I couldn't keep the tip of the rod up. There was a snap as the leader broke. The rod swung up and the pull was gone.

For the first time I realized I was up to my hips in the cold water. It took me a long time to get the line reeled back in. I had smashed through a whole bed of mint along the edge of the creek and the smell was all around me.

I didn't know how long Dad had been calling me. He was standing on the hillside against the sky and couldn't see me.

I yelled and ran to him. He pointed his finger at me but I cut him off. "I had a big trout on! More than two feet long I bet. So big I couldn't keep the rod up and it broke the leader."

Dad smiled. "Well, he'll still be there next year. Maybe you can catch him then."

"Next year?"

"Sure. Big trout don't move around that much."

It was the kind of thing I didn't understand. How could anybody think that far ahead about something?

While we walked up the old hillroad, he told me how he had fished in Norway, when he was a boy, for the big salmon that came back from the sea and went into the narrow fjords on their way upstream to spawn.

"People claim the same ones keep coming back," Dad said. "Always in the early fall, back to the same stream they came from."

"You mean they're just going home?"

"I suppose you could say that."

"Well, how do they know to do that."

"I guess nobody's figured that out. My God, I never saw fish like that again."

We stopped to rest near the top of the hill, the valley spread out below us. Harvey Shields' house was on the far side of the creek, still open to the light in the southwestern sky. Somebody was out in the yard, split-

ting wood. We could see the axe swing and fall. Because of the distance,
the axe was swinging up again before the sound reached us. It was a
woman, a big one, so it had to be Harvey's mother.

"Hey," I said, "I didn't know she ever came out of the house."

"I guess she's got to with Harvey gone."

"Where'd he go?"

"Why, we were talking about it at the table. Weren't you there?
Sunday before last she woke up and he was gone. Left a note saying he was
going on a trip. I'd say he's not back yet either or she wouldn't be out there
splitting wood."

I could see the old road curving out of sight, the point of the hill
hiding the bridge where I'd gone in the ditch that night. The sound of the
axe came a last time, after the woman had bent down to pick up a piece of
wood. I almost told Dad I had seen Harvey that night, but I didn't know
any way to do it without getting in trouble for being on that road.

Sunday. That meant Harvey had left the morning after I had seen
him, or even that same night. Maybe he had gone right home, written his
note and headed out, looking for some other bridge to slide across, or for
that girl in Minnesota who would look twenty years older than the way he
remembered.

We went on up the hillroad and into the dark woods. Dad didn't
talk anymore. It was always that way. Something would remind him of the
Old Country, as he called it, he would talk for a minute and then pull back
inside himself again. I suddenly realized I didn't know much about him,
except for what I learned by going through the old brown suitcase full of
pictures, some from Norway, some from America in the days before he
met Mom. A lot of the pictures were of him with different young girls, and
some of girls by themselves, each in a long dress and gloves and usually
smiling. There was something funny about it. In the pictures, those girls
weren't much older than I was and now the man who had known them was
my father.

We walked the rest of the way home without him saying anything
more. He tousled my hair when we got to the house. He hadn't done that
for a long time. I guess he forgot about bawling me out for not coming

home from the creek "before your mother starts to worry." He stood there smiling at me, his hand on my head. I thought about Anne. I almost asked if he ever wondered about any of those girls in the pictures. I couldn't think of a way to say it and in a minute the chance was gone.

"Maybe next year," he said.

He was still thinking about the big trout.

Because of the fly-fishing I forgot all about making sure I had some way of getting to Elaine's on Saturday night. Lars and Erik took me as far as Three Corners. Everybody seemed to be going in another direction until I linked up with the going steady couple. Willy and Marge were about as interesting as a mashed potato sandwich but it was better than nothing.

"Can't promise I'll find us a cow rodeo," Willy said, grinning. Marge didn't even say hello.

When Elaine saw who was in the car, she made a face at me. "Sorry," I whispered.

It was the first time we had ever been in a back seat together. Elaine kept looking at me as though I might suddenly grab her and she stayed way over on her side, with just our hands touching in the middle of the seat. Willy was whistling through his teeth, Marge sitting close to him, neither of them saying anything, and we rode like that all the way to Indian Springs.

The dance hall was warm and half dark, the band a quiet one with the saxaphone player doing his best to make everybody cry. We danced without talking, hardly noticing when the music ended and started again, just staying close to each other. Elaine's dress was damp in the back and I could feel the straps underneath. Whenever I saw Willy and Marge, they were dancing the same way, Willy looking down at her, his face red and sweating. She was always staring off at nothing.

At intermission, we went over to Jake's. His face lighted up and he came out from behind the bar to our booth. "Hey, you two! Good to see you. Where's your crazy friend?"

"Gone out West to work in the wheat harvest," I said.

Jake went to get our drinks.

"I didn't know he'd already gone," Elaine said. "Why didn't you say anything?" She was staring at me and I didn't know what she was thinking.

"He just left this week."

Jake was back, beaming at us. "Been over to the dance?"

"Yes."

"I used to do that. One summer it rained every Saturday night and the lights went out every time. It was one of those lucky summers. I was dancing with exactly the right girl every time it happened."

A man at the bar laughed. "The way I remember it, Jake. Every girl in town was exactly the right one sometime or another."

"Yeah, Jake. What about that one lived up above the drug store? Remember the time her folks came home unexpected and you got tangled up with her little brother's coaster wagon and rode it down the stairs?"

"Shut up," Jake said. He was still smiling at us. "Did seem like every pretty girl in the country was around here that one summer. I guess you two don't have to worry about looking for anybody. You're all you need."

We went back to the dance and everything was just the way it had been before. We started home and everything in the car was the same, too, but when we got away from the lights of town, I pulled Elaine over to me, not being very careful where I touched her. For a minute she kissed me back. Then she went all still and I was kissing somebody who wasn't even there. I let her go and slumped into the corner of the seat. She turned her back and leaned against me, her head on my shoulder. My arms were around her and she held my hands still.

Above her head I could see out the window. The moon was shining. There was fog in the narrow hollows, filling the road in places, so thick that Willy had to slow down. I remembered coming home from town at night when I was younger, and how Dad would speed up the motor of the Model-T Ford, brightening the headlights so he could see where to turn onto the road leading up to our ridge. The fog was often thick that way when summer was moving close to fall.

"You've been away," Elaine said.

I guess it was the second time she'd said it. She had turned in my arms and was looking at me. I hadn't noticed her do that. I pulled her close and just held her.

At Elaine's house, Willy got out with us, pretending to look at the front tires. He grabbed my arm and let Elaine get ahead. "Take your time. You waited for me last time. Anyway, I need every chance I can get, too."

He let go of my arm, then grabbed it again. "Hey, you got something?"

"No."

He pushed something soft and smooth into my hand. "Here. I got more. Not that I've needed any so far."

I put it in my pocket and followed Elaine. She was standing under the pine tree. A cool breeze was moving the needles. She hugged herself and stared up into the trees.

She wants to go back to start again, I thought.

She turned around and watched me as I came close, still hugging herself, the moonlight full on her face and she looked sad. I had never seen her quite that way before. I put my hands out and tried to turn the corners of her mouth up and make her smile. She didn't pull away, even turned her cheek so it was against my hand, but she didn't smile.

"Elaine, what's the matter?"

She shivered, arms tight around herself. "I don't know. Tomorrow morning my parents are going to ask what I did last night. They always do. I always say 'Oh, nothing much.' This time for a change it'll be the truth."

I felt the cold now myself and wanted to yell something that would hurt her. I took a deep breath. "Aw, come on, Elaine. It's just being with those two."

"Maybe that's how we'll be looking to everybody else pretty soon."

She half turned away. I could hardly hear the rest of what she said. "If there is a pretty soon."

I tried to turn her so she would look at me, my hands on her shoulders. She kept swinging her head away. When I put my hand up to her face, I found out she was crying.

She whirled. "You know the only good thing that happened tonight? It was Jake! When he looked at us he was seeing somebody special! And we are!"

She turned her face away again. "Or were."

She ran to the door and was inside before I could catch up. I couldn't see her and there wasn't a sound, but I was pretty sure she was there just inside the door.

"Elaine?"

She didn't answer.

"If I can get the car, I'll come by tomorrow."

I went back to the pine tree and waited there to give Willy his chance. I heard a sound toward the house. I thought it was footsteps and she was coming back, but it was only the damn dog thumping. I'd forgotten to pet him. I felt like going back and kicking him instead.

I waited a little longer, then started whistling to let Willy know I was coming. He got out and came part way to meet me, pulling his clothes straight.

"How'd you do?" I asked.

"Close. Very close. You?"

"No."

"I heard her yelling something. She sure is emotional."

Where the road came near the creek below our farm, I told Willy to stop. "I'll walk the rest of the way."

"You sure?"

"Yeah."

I was sitting in front, with Marge in the middle. She turned and said "Why?"

Her voice startled me. It didn't seem possible, but it was the first thing I had heard her say all night. For once she wasn't smiling and it seemed almost as if there might be somebody in there.

"I like being in the woods at night."

"That might be fun." She leaned back and started smiling again.

I watched the taillights fade into the fog and had the whole valley to myself. The grade school was just across the creek. I walked over and sat in the swing, going back and forth slowly, the squeaking muffled in the fog, the seat wet under me. I tried to pull Elaine back close to me and she kept slipping away.

In a minute, I told myself, I'm going up to the safe ridgetop world of the farm and be just plain old Steve Carlson again and not have to worry about somebody wanting me to be someone else.

"Damnit!" I yelled. "I already don't know who I am!"

I listened, hearing water dripping somewhere, but there wasn't even an echo to argue with.

After a while I went into the schoolhouse through a basement window and tiptoed around in the darkness of the one big room with its bolted-down desks. I couldn't believe the silence, then realized I had never been there before when the big clock at the front wasn't going, seeming to tick about once every five minutes in the late afternoon. I wound and set the clock and started the pendulum going.

Then I crowded into the desk that had been mine in the eighth grade, and listened to the slow tick-tock. I could remember every desk I had sat in during my journey from one side of the room to the other, each desk one grade too small for my legs.

A girl from the next valley had been next to me the last year. Once, on a nature walk, the teacher asked me to get an empty oriole's nest from high up in a tree. That girl, who had never seemed to notice me before, stood down below, upturned face worried, and she said, "Oh, Steve, please be careful." But when I came down, and accidently rolled a rock toward the others, she looked up along the hillside and said "Smart aleck," and was all cold again even if she was very pretty.

I couldn't remember anything else about her. My God, I thought, I'm getting as bad as the Oldest Man in the World. "Let's see now, what was her name? Delores, maybe? Or was that her sister's name?"

I squeezed out of the seat, found some chalk and began printing on the blackboard.

"Beyond grade school there be tigers."

"It's girls who don't know what girls are for!"

"But that was in another country and besides the wench is dead."

I started to leave but came back up the stairs and erased the board. There was going to be a school district meeting in a few days. It would be better just to let people wonder about the clock ticking away in the summer.

T he next day when Lars and I pulled into the ballfield in Gordon's Landing, I didn't just ask him for the car. I said I had to have it. "That same girl?" he asked.

"Yes."

"You have a fight with her?"

I hadn't thought about it being a fight, but that was better than not knowing what was going on. "I guess so."

"All right. Just remember we have to get back for chores. Erik might forget to come home." Lars laughed because I had told Erik about the big trout and he had been spending all his spare time trying to catch it.

Elaine was sitting under the pine tree when I pulled in. She ran to the car, got in and slid over close to me in a way that made me sure there was no one else at home. She was wearing bluejeans and a dusty-blue shirt the same color as her eyes. I had been all ready to cheer her up, but she was looking as pretty as I'd ever seen her, all eager and ready to take on the world.

"About last night."

She put a finger against my lips. "I've decided not to think about last night."

She was kneeling on the seat, her face near mine. I pulled out of there quickly, getting away from the empty house before I did something crazy, not even daring to look at her until we got down to the main road. The fence row at the intersection was lined with asters. We sat and laughed at the way the flower stems were bowing under the weight of bumble bees, dumping them down into the grass where they thrashed their way up to try again.

Elaine was still sitting close to me and humming to herself as we turned down the valley. I kept glancing at her, trying to figure out what was different. Each time, she smiled and moved a little against me.

Where the river road crossed a creek, I pulled in and parked.

"Come on," I said.

I took her hand and led her into the willows, then upstream to a place where there were poplar stumps with piles of chips around them. We sat on a log and I pointed to the edge of the stream. "Watch."

In a few minutes there was a sound from upstream. A moving V started toward us. "There," I whispered.

"What is it?"

"Beaver."

It slid onto the bank, eyes right on us once before it moved to a fallen poplar and began gnawing, so close we could hear its teeth and the sound of chips falling. A sharp slap came from downstream. The beaver slipped into the water without a sound and stayed under.

"Will it come back?" Elaine whispered.

"Not right away."

She was looking at me, thinking something that made her frown. "I never saw one before. What happened?"

"Another beaver slapped its tail on the water as a warning. Something scared it, down by the road."

She went on looking at me that way, still not saying whatever it was she kept thinking. I had been trying not to touch her, but now my hand seemed to move out all by itself and rest on her knee. She put her hand over mine.

"I like this," she said. "Being here, like this."

I didn't trust myself to move. From upstream where the creek came down over a riffle, I could hear the rattling call of a kingfisher. Elaine took a deep breath and put her head way back. I could feel the warmth of her shoulder. My hand tightened on her knee and was about to start moving whether I wanted it to or not. I pulled my hand away and got up. It was time to get out of there if I was going to try being who she seemed to want me to be. Going back to the car, I let her walk ahead, afraid she would see what she was doing to me.

In Gordon's Landing I waved to the Oldest Man in the World, but drove right on through and had pulled halfway into the parking lot of the Hole in the Wall before I realized the place was gone. It had burned down. There were just the three concrete steps now, weeds already growing up around them, leading into a pile of blackened rubble. We sat there staring at it and I had a feeling I had gone to sleep and a lot of things had happened while I was away.

"For God's sake! How come nobody told us?"

"We haven't talked to anybody lately," Elaine said.

She got out of the car and walked over to the steps where the shadflies had been an inch thick that night. I walked the other way, to the slough. The water was low and the shoreline was drying up and had a strong mud-flat smell. Standing beside the old rowboats that had been pulled out of the water some fall and forgotten, I tried to figure out why it bothered me so much that the Hole in the Wall had burned down. There was a fresh supply of empty beer cans scattered all over the parking lot so the place was still an X on Bottles' map.

Elaine was sitting on the top step, elbows on her knees, chin resting in her hands. I went over and sat down on the warm concrete beside her. She didn't seem to know I was there.

I touched her shoulder. "What's the matter?"

She shook her head. "I don't know. It makes it seem like a million years."

I laughed. "It was only a couple months ago."

"No it wasn't."

She turned to me for a moment, the blue eyes very bright, then looked over her shoulder at what used to be the Hole in the Wall. There was a little pulse beating at the side of her throat and her chin had a stubborn set that again reminded me of Billy talking about being the oldest man in the world someday.

She went on staring, shaking her head. "Any minute now," she said, "it's going to start over. With the jukebox playing 'It Makes No Difference Now.' Or maybe not. Maybe a different song this time."

One of those rabbit-hopped-over-my-grave chills went through me. All at once she was somebody I didn't know. She even looked different, her face older and more angled, eyes shadowed and mysterious, and her mouth curved in something that wasn't a smile at all.

"My God, you were young that night."

She nodded. "I thought you said it was only two months."

The sun had gone behind the hill to the southwest. There was a beginning feel of evening in the air. Frogs should have been calling in the slough, but there wasn't a sound.

I picked up an empty beer can and threw it as hard as I could, liking the clatter it made. "We've almost used them up!"

"Used what up?" She was looking at me with a frown again.

"The X's."

Held away from her by the idea of the game, I looked her over and she was just breasts, legs, hips.

Some color came into her face. "We've used them all up except one."

She was still looking at me that way and I wasn't sure if she had really said it or if I was inside her mind again the way I had been the night we met. For the first time, I noticed how tanned her face was. There were some little veins showing at her temples, slight shadows against the brown. I had never seen them before.

"You seem different," I said.

"Don't forget I'm seventeen now."

"Hey, you said you'd tell me what you wished."

"I said maybe." Her eyes went over my face. "I wish. . . ."

She suddenly leaned forward and put her hands on my shoulders, biting her lips, wanting to say something, but waiting as though she thought I should already know.

"Steve. . . . Steve, couldn't. . . ."

"What?"

She went on staring, still expecting something from me and I couldn't get inside her mind to find out what it was.

"Nothing." She shook her head and turned, kneeling on the top step, looking in at the pipes sticking up where the bar had been. Her back was to me. I watched her, thinking how rounded and smooth she was and could feel my hands wanting to reach out and slide down along her.

I moved away from her, down to the bottom step, trying to see her the way she had been that first night when it all seemed so simple. Or had that night been filled with X's, too? The look of her in the white dress. A touch on the arm. Taking the shadfly out of her hair. The pine tree and the kiss. Had it already been happening, moving from one ultimate to another and nothing we could do once it started?

"Let's get out of here!"

"All right," she said.

When I got into the car, I started to glance once more at the place and she said, "Don't look!"

I had never heard her say anything that sharply before. "What are you talking about?"

She was staring straight through me. "I don't know."

I drove out of there, tires crunching over empty beer cans, and turned up the river road. We drove through Gordon's Landing without saying anything. I would have gone right past Elm Springs, too, if I hadn't noticed the sign. When I saw that, I pulled in. It was on a shiny, new steel post beside the spring and it said "Unsafe for Human Consumption."

"Well for God's sake!"

"What's the matter?"

I pointed to the sign. "Everything's going to hell at once."

I hadn't driven past Elm Springs since the last time I looked for Anne. The door of the shack was open and a couple of windows were smashed in. It was all at once some kind of a bad dream where you know all the time it's a dream, but at the same time know you're never going to wake up in time to save yourself.

Elaine touched my face. "Hey, what's going on?"

"I knew a girl here once."

"What happened?"

I remembered the Oldest Man in the World. "I let her get away from me. At least I think I did. Bottles said I just made her up."

"Did you?"

"I don't know anymore. I just never found out what happened. My God, I even hitched to La Crosse once, trying to find her."

Elaine sighed. "We are all looking in distance for things that are lost somewhere in time." She seemed to be reciting it.

"Who said that?"

"Bottles. That night at Indian Springs. I tried to write a poem about it."

"I didn't know you wrote poetry."

"There's a lot you don't know."

"What does that mean?"

"About me."

"I do know you!"

"No you don't!"

I felt the way I did when I argued with my parents. I even had my head reared back the way Mom always said I did when I was being stubborn.

"Maybe we're too young," Elaine said.

"Too young for what?"

"For what we do to each other."

I laughed. "What's that?"

She whirled around on the seat. "Damn you, stop it! Don't treat me like some little fluff-head who doesn't know anything. I live on a farm, remember? I know all about bulls and cows. I've seen them doing it to each other. But I'm not a cow! I'm a girl, remember?"

She was crying, tears running down and she didn't cover up her face, but sat straight up, staring at me, daring me to say one wrong word.

She took a deep breath. "I'm sorry I yelled at you."

"Elaine . . . Aw hell, Elaine, I don't even know what's going on most of the time. This damn place. That girl's name was Anne. The first time I saw her she was standing on the path with a bucket of water from the spring. . . ."

I told Elaine everything about the night of the excursion. She had her arms around me, holding me and I told her how I kept coming back to look for Anne. I was crying. I didn't know if Elaine knew it or not. She held me and we sat that way for a long time.

"This is what I wished," Elaine said.

"What?"

"This."

The sun was coming in low over the river and I knew we had to go or I would be in trouble with Lars. I drove Elaine home and she stayed close against me, her hand on my shoulder. At her house, I could hear voices from inside and there was just time to pull her to me for a moment and kiss her. Time for me to feel her breasts against me and want to do more than just hold her.

I pulled back. "See you Saturday night, OK? It's the fair."

"All right."

20

Next morning I went back to being part of the farm, working harder than anyone expected, perspiration making white salt rings on my clothes, the screaming of dogday flies going higher and higher, cutting straight through my head.

One day when we finished haying early, I ran full speed along the ridge to the south, falling at the edge of the woods when my legs would carry me no farther. A fox squirrel was tearing open a corn husk in the field we called "the new ground," and I remembered when that land had been my favorite playground, with thick hazel brush, openings filled with violets in the spring and, later, shooting stars and the bright red of Indian paintbrush. Now it was just a cornfield, absolutely motionless in the hot sun.

A pileated woodpecker began tearing apart a dead limb above my head, the pieces falling on me, and I knew exactly why it had to do that.

From deeper in the woods there was a rattling sound. I crept toward it. Dry dirt was landing on fallen leaves. The digging animal was gray and big and I thought it might be a last timber wolf. It whirled, growling, teeth bared, hair standing up along its back, then leaped away and ran down into the hollow. It was a coyote and the wolves that had howled there were gone, their deep voices more a feeling now than remembered sound.

No birds were singing. A slight breeze came up along the hillside, carrying the smell of old leaves. I waited. Something was there. Not just all the one-by-one things, but a gathering of it into a whole that tried to speak to me with its silence.

The bell began ringing, telling me supper was ready. I ran out of the woods, a meadow lark running ahead of me in the hayfield, dragging one wing, leading me away from its nest. I chased it, made it fly, then ran home and slid into my chair just in time to hear Dad say, "I thought we would all take tomorrow off."

"How come?"

"Your mother and I are going to a funeral."

"Do we have to go?" Lars asked.

"No."

"Good!" Erik said.

The three of us hated funerals, but Mom and Dad were always going to them, and weddings, too, seeming to enjoy one as much as the other.

"How come," I said, "there are so many more funerals than weddings?"

"Why, I guess you need two people for a wedding and only one for a funeral," Dad said. He patted me on the head and everyone laughed.

"Well, how come you like funerals so much?"

Mom looked surprised. "Maybe because it seems that's the only time people get together and have a chance to talk to each other."

"It's a little late for the one who died."

She laughed. "Yes, it is, isn't it. I guess we should have our funerals while we're alive. We'd get to see people we hadn't seen in years."

She was smiling. Lars looked disgusted. Erik's mind was off somewhere else, probably thinking about tomorrow, and Dad was laughing. I looked at them, one by one. It was the first time I had thought about maybe going to their funerals someday.

Next morning we watched the car leave, the three of us looking at each other and grinning, maybe all thinking the same thing. When we were younger the disappearing car had been a signal to do all the forbidden things — fill our pockets with matches, climb the windmill tower, start the pump engine and tie the governor down to see how fast it would run.

"I'm going fishing," Erik said.

"I'm going to sleep," Lars said.

They looked at me and Lars laughed. "Too bad you don't have a car. You could go see that girl. You patch up your fight with her?"

"I think so."

I went to the creek with Erik. He headed right for the hole with the big trout and we sat on the bank, dangling our feet in the water, catching a few chubs.

Downstream a bunch of mud hens seemed to be practicing take-offs, taxiing along the water, wings thrashing, feet splashing. Instead of taking off, they would crash into the bank at the end of the pool, then go back to try again.

When the sun had gone around to the south, we went to the old orchard, ate our sandwiches, then gathered a pile of the ripest apples and lay on our backs, eating carefully around the worm holes.

I could see the down of thistle seeds riding up along the hillside, turned silver in the sunlight, disappearing as they were caught and carried off by the northwest wind.

"Boy, don't you wish you could ride the wind like that, going to all kinds of places you've never been before?"

"What places?"

"I don't know. Just places with all kinds of things happening."

"I like it right here," Erik said. He bit into another apple, then took the bite out of his mouth to check it.

"Hell, isn't there anything you want to do?"

"What's wrong with what we're doing right now?"

"Aw, come on, Erik. There's got to be something."

He carefully worked at the apple. "You'd laugh at me."

"No I won't."

"All right. I want to invent a tractor. A radio controlled kind that runs all by itself, with nobody on it."

"What good will that do?"

"It can pull a mower behind it to cut the hay. And behind the mower a machine I'll invent will in a few seconds make the hay just right to put in. And behind that a hay baler with a chute that puts the bales on a wagon so all you have to do is stop once in awhile to change wagons."

I could see that train of machinery winding halfway across our farm, dropping into ditches, running through fences and going wild down the steep hills.

"Can you send the loaded wagon off to the barn by itself, too?"

Erik smiled. "I'm working on that."

I remembered the time he had rigged up a spring-driven motor to turn the cream separator, taking the place of the hand cranking long enough for him to run to the well for a cold drink. It worked fine until Dad gave the thing a pull to see what it was and the spring came out and thrashed around the milkhouse for about five minutes.

"When you going to do all this inventing?"

"When I get around to it."

I could hear chopping from across the valley. It was Harvey Shields' mother again. She was getting better at it, the swings of the axe coming in a steady, echoing rhythm.

"I didn't know you had a girl," Erik said.

"Well, I guess I do."

"What do you talk about?"

"About anything. Sometimes not about anything."

"I don't think I'd know what to talk about. I mean what girl's going to be interested in my tractor that goes all by itself?"

"Maybe they would."

"I think they'd think I'm crazy."

"I don't think you're crazy."

"You're a brother. Brothers don't mind people being crazy."

"Well, haven't you ever had a girl?"

"There was one in high school I kind of liked."

"Why don't you ever go out with her?"

"I don't know."

"Well she might be gone by the time you get ready."

"Yeah, I know. There'll be others when I get around to it."

I raised up on my elbow to look at him because I didn't believe it, but he was still eating away on an apple, looking up at the sky as if he didn't have a care in the world.

On our way home the woods were filled with the screaming of dog-day flies. Toward evening the day went silent for an hour or two, then the katydids started their over and over again wing scraping — rasp-rasp, rasp-rasp, rasp-rasp.

I woke in the night and the sound was still there. I had been dreaming about Elaine. There was no beginning, but I remembered pieces. We were at the big flat rock. Then down in the meadow. Tigers paced and growled at the edge of the woods. Suddenly it was evening. Red and gold light outlined her breasts, the curve of her hips. We were hidden in the grass. A wind sighed through it, saying the season was ending. Her legs were stretched out. I ran my hand along them. I could feel myself getting ready and I remembered saying, "What would you do if I did that?"

"Did what?"

"Grabbed you. Pushed you down. Made it happen."

The tigers stopped pacing and waited. The wind wasn't moving the grass. She sat up straight and stared at me.

I jumped up from my bed because I didn't want to hear her answer again. The katydids all seemed to be right outside my window screen — rasp-rasp, rasp-rasp. I pulled on my clothes, crawled out and ran down the lane into the woods. In the dry ditch I picked up rocks and threw them up into the trees, yelling "Shut up! Shut up!"

The katydids paused, then went right on — rasp-rasp, rasp-rasp.

I ran into the woods, following our old path toward the log cabin. Even before I got there I noticed the candle smell, but there was no light coming through the windows.

I pushed open the door and was suddenly shivering.

"Is somebody there?"

There wasn't a sound from inside. I struck a match and checked the candle on the table. The wax was soft and warm. A screech owl called, down toward the spring. I went to the door and looked into the night.

"It's all right," I called. "You can use the cabin."

I closed the door and ran home and looked through Erik's window. His bed was empty.

Back in my own room, I tried to keep from falling asleep because I didn't want the dream to come back. In the dream when I said that to Elaine, I remembered how she stared at me a long time, looking exactly the way she had when she said she knew about bulls and cows and had seen them doing it to each other. And finally she answered.

"If you did that to me I would say 'Moo!'"

I stayed awake a long time, listening to the katydids. I never heard a sound from Erik's room.

21

The weather changed in the night. On Saturday morning a cold wind blew out of the north and I could imagine the men at Gordon's Landing interrupting their talk about girls, the Oldest Man in the World pulling his jacket tighter, saying "Kind of day makes you wonder what you did with your summer's wages."

All day I watched the sun, wanting it to move faster so I could get off the ridge to someplace where things were happening. After evening chores, when I was getting ready, I got Willy's condom out of hiding and put it in my wallet.

Elaine was wearing a coat with a fur collar. Even before she got in the car I was wondering what it would be like to put my hands under the coat and find her. I pulled out and turned toward the valley. As she slid over to me, closer than usual, I noticed her perfume.

"Hey, you smell good."

She laughed and buried her face in the fur collar. "Partly that's to hide the mothballs."

With her head down and eyes turned sideways toward me, she was like a picture of a pretty girl in a magazine ad, mysterious and happy, ready for anything.

"I had a dream about you last night," I said.

"What kind of dream?"

I told her, but only up to the point where I began touching her legs. "And there must have been flowers in the meadow," I said. "I just remembered the smell of asters."

She was half smiling, part of her face still covered, seeming to be daring me to find her in there. Instead of asters I started remembering the rubbery smell of the condom.

"I think there was more to the dream," she said.

"Yes."

"You're not going to tell me?"

"No." I knew my face was getting red.

She leaned back and laughed at me, but stayed close and I wondered what she would do if I told her the rest..

Music from the merry-go-round came to meet us at the fair grounds. We ran toward the midway, holding hands. Rides were whirling, people yelling, the smell of hotdogs and hamburgers in the air, loudspeaker voices echoing off the buildings, and both of us were looking around like ten year-olds.

For awhile we just walked, staying in step, pushed close to each other in the crowd and I could feel her moving against me all the way from shoulders to legs. I put my arm around her, not under the coat yet, afraid she would pull away. I felt her arm go around me and we went on walking, holding each other.

The crowd carried us to a tent with a big sign that said "MYSTERIOUS UNIDENTIFIED CREATURE!" A man with a cowboy hat was yelling "Head like a fox! Tail like a monkey! International scientists baffled!"

We went in. The animal was in a cage, acting scared to death and it did have a long tail and a fox-like face. I looked closely and started laughing.

"Pardon me," I said, bowing to Elaine, "I'm international scientist Dr. Carlson and what we have here is a Madagascar lemur, its name in Latin meaning 'ghost' I believe."

Elaine was staring at me. Everyone in the tent had turned to look. The man with the cowboy hat grabbed our arms and ushered us out, smiling broadly and at the same time whispering, "One more word and I'll wring your neck!" He was a big man.

Elaine was beginning to laugh.

The man took us outside, gave me back our money, and said "Get lost!"

"That's no way to treat an international scientist," I said.

He laughed. "Is that what the damn thing is?"

"I think so. I did a project about lemurs for biology last year."

He went back into the tent.

Elaine was laughing so hard she could hardly walk. We stopped and she leaned against me, trying to get her breath. Then she reached up, standing on tiptoe, put both arms around my neck and kissed me. I felt about ten feet tall.

We started on the rides — the death-defying pendulum, the whirling octopus, the airplane cockpit where money fell out of pockets when riders hung upside down. We kept grabbing each other and I didn't have to be careful where I touched her as the rides threw us together, pulled us apart, threw us together again.

When we lined up for the shake-em-up ride, the hair on the girl in front of us was sticking out in all directions. It was Eva Mae, with a boy who was sunburned bright red except for where his hair had just been cut.

"Hey," she said. "You never came back to break those blue glass things."

"No. I never did, did I?"

The boy pulled her onto the ride and I watched her, feeling I had lost something.

Elaine gave my arm a nudge. "Old girl friend?"

"Just somebody's sister. She went on a picnic with us once."

"All right." Elaine was looking at me as though she knew all about that day.

We crowded up close to the stage, still touching, moving a little with the music. A group played "Turkey in the Straw," feet clomping up and down. A woman in a white hat sang a song that began "I can laugh about it now, but sometimes I still want to cry."

I threw baseballs at wooden milk bottles and won two bright red walking canes with yellow tassels on the knobs. We walked with them, taking long strides, holding on to each other. People kept turning to look at us, maybe because we were laughing a lot. Each time I took out my wallet to pay for something, the condom was right there.

We threw rings at prizes fastened to wooden blocks, the man yelling "Hey, Hey, Hey! Watch the young gentleman get a present for his little lady!"

I won a kewpie doll with bright orange hair and gave it to Elaine. "Here you are, Little Lady."

The smell of hamburgers hit us and we looked at each other and nodded. As we crowded into the warm, steamy tent, a man in a chef's cap called "Get your hotdogs while they're hot. Some with mustard, some with not!"

We had trouble with the ketchup and he yelled, "Shake, oh shake the bottle! First none'll come and then a lot'll!"

When we finished, I reached out to wipe some red off Elaine's face. "You've got 'lot'll' on your chin," I said, having to yell in the racket.

She smiled and said something that sounded like "I love you, too." But she wouldn't say it again.

A crying little girl grabbed Elaine's legs and held tight. Elaine knelt down and put her arms around the girl, looking at me over her head, with an expression I had never seen before. She was so pretty I couldn't stand it.

A man pulled the girl away, and she looked back over her shoulder, wiggling her fingers at us. I lifted Elaine up, hands under her arms, not wanting to let go.

We ran to the merry-go-round and got on two side-by-side horses, the music so loud we couldn't talk, our hands touching, Elaine's horse coming up each time mine was going down.

The Ferris wheel stopped and left us suspended at the exact top, where no one could see us. The wind was blowing and Elaine's skirt kept lifting. I reached out to help her hold it down and left my hand in her lap. By tipping forward, we could see people down below, looking strange as they walked.

"I don't understand what holds them up," Elaine said, laughing.

I rocked the seat back and forth. She let go of her skirt and grabbed onto me. Her face was cool. I went on rocking the seat and kissing her.

When we came down, the crowd was thinning, some of the tents being torn down. We had a hotdog, our hands bumping into each other every time we reached for anything. Elaine nudged me and pointed. The Funniest Woman in the World was sitting on the running board of a truck, chin in her hands, looking very sad, while a recording of her laughter played behind her.

I was afraid everything was going to change. I led Elaine out of the food tent and we ran to the parking lot, swinging our canes.

The car was covered with dew. Inside, we were in a private world where no one could see us. I reached for her, kissing her, trying to get my hands under the coat, and finally she took my hands and put them on the steering wheel, laughing as she did that.

She stayed close to me as we pulled out, on a road that wound through a narrow hollow, then climbed steeply to the ridge. When we reached the top, a long line of fire was creeping along the curve of the hillside, the flames low, smoke coming to us with the smell of burning grass and oak leaves. Someone had been burning off a pasture, counting on the night dampness to put it out.

I parked the car. We ran to the fire and it was like being at the fair again as we raced along the line of flames, one on each side, our hands meeting in the middle, with sparks and partly burned leaves floating up, the leaf edges smoldering outlines of deep, glowing orange.

The smoke stung our eyes, tears washing streaks on our faces.

Elaine let go of my hand and ran back the way we had come. I jumped across the line of flames to catch her and she jumped to the side I had been on. Each time I reached for her, she got away. My eyes were so full of smoke I couldn't see her some of the time. She would come up while I was rubbing them, touch me and run off before I could grab her. Then I would see her on the other side of the flames, laughing at me, her hair orange in the light, face smudged.

The line of fire moved farther down the hillside. Elaine stopped running. I put my arms around her and held her tight, feeling her breathing, smelling the smoke in her hair. My face was burning from the heat and smoke.

We walked back, arms around each other, feet making little puffs in the ashes. I opened the car door. I wasn't sure but it seemed to me she hesitated, and I swung the front seat forward. She looked at me and for a moment I was certain she was going to say "Moo."

She didn't. She got in the back and turned, waiting for me, still breathing deeply from our running, flames lighting her face, her coat open so my arms went inside it, finding her. Nothing had ever been that warm before and there was no turning back.

The flickering light from the fire was almost gone and the smell of the ashes was strong and acrid as the dew settled. In the quiet, I had that same empty feeling I got whenever I thought of the girl at High Ridge or of Anne. Then I was walking along the creek in the early evening, crushing mint with my feet, reaching under rocks, feeling the arching trout in my hands before I let it go.

Elaine stirred in my arms, looking at me, face very still.

I raised up so I could see out. The line of fire was moving very slowly, far down the hillside, the flames low. I watched them, remembering a night Erik and I had found a fire burning that way on the bald hills down toward the Kickapoo Valley. We ran to get closer, led on by sudden bursts of brighter flame as the fire touched off caches of dry leaves. We ran along its length on the steep hillside, then started home, running at first to tell Dad it was headed away from our land and was almost surely going to burn itself out soon. Then, almost home, we stopped and looked at each other, deciding without saying a word what we were going to do, each thinking of food, because that was what we were always thinking of if ten minutes had passed since we had eaten. We crept into the yard, opened the smokehouse door slowly to keep the hinges from squeaking and took one of the cloth bags of smoked sausage. We ran back, downhill all the way, cut thick slices and roasted them on forked sticks above the moving line of fire. Erik was covered with fine, gray ashes and looked like somebody in a school play made up to be an old, old man.

"You've been away," Elaine was saying.

"No."

"Yes, you've been away."

"No I haven't."

"Yes. Like a little boy gone chasing dragon flies."

"What are you talking about?"

"A poem. He never came back."

"I'm right here," I said. I thought of the first night, seeing her looking up at the pine tree and remembered the rush of feelings when everything was so new. I wanted to tell her about that feeling, say all the things I was thinking and that it was going to be all right because now we were closer together and I would be able to talk to her.

I pulled her close so I could tell her and felt tears in my eyes because she was Elaine. I cupped her face in my hands, feeling the warmth, smelling the smoke from our skin and the words didn't come out. She smiled a little and turned her head, putting her lips against my palm. I let my hands drop down to her shoulders, my fingers making a rustling sound as I moved them lower, the words getting farther and farther away. I touched her breasts. I heard her breath catch, but she didn't pull back, just shook her head, the smile gone. Her face had a funny, empty expression. And even before her lips moved I knew she was going to say the same thing again.

"You've been away, Steve."

She was still staring at me in that funny way and she was somebody I had never seen before.

"If you could go away now, you'll do that again. We don't really know each other. . . . Maybe it was too soon. Or even not soon enough. I don't know. . . . Or because we did it at all. . . ."

She took a deep breath. I could feel her moving under my hands.

"Maybe we happened too young. Now we can't happen to each other when we should. . . . Because we've used each other up."

I jerked my eyes away. The words were too old. They weren't even part of me, as strange as her talking about not knowing if something was lost or just not yet found, or Anne saying, on that last day, "We only get one chance at anything."

I pulled my hands away.

Elaine got out of the car and stood a minute, pulling her clothes straight, staring toward the retreating fire. I saw her arm swing. A little powdery puff of ashes rose as whatever she threw landed in the burned-over ground. Then she got into the front seat.

When I stopped the car at her house, I tried to put my arms around her, but she pulled away and got out and went up the walk ahead of me. At the door, she let me hold her, her head against my chest so that when she spoke, all I could hear were the words "met you."

I lifted her face. She was crying. "You wish you'd never met me?"

"I wish I had."

She pulled away, went inside and hooked the screendoor.

"Good night, Elaine."

She had already gone. I walked down the path, remembering to step over the dog, and reached out to touch the pine tree. My hand came away sticky with the strong smelling pitch. No light came on in the house. The windmill wasn't turning. Even the katydids were silent. The night had a cold stillness that said frost was coming.

22

Next morning I remembered the kewpie doll I had given to Elaine. She hadn't been carrying it when she went to the door. I checked the car, but it wasn't there. Then I knew what it was she had thrown toward the fire.

I could feel my face puckering up. I ran to the house, grabbed a bucket and ran out again, yelling back that I was going to look for blackberries. Mom came to the door and called something after me, but I was running fast and couldn't hear. I ran all the way down into the hollow to a place where the berry vines arched over the damp ditch, with tall red oaks leaning in to shade them from both sides. The berries were there, despite the dryness and heat of the summer.

I crowded my way in among the long canes, jerking loose when they wrapped around me, the briars scratching, some of them breaking off and staying in my skin in neat rows with blood seeping out around them. I kept grabbing the berries, fighting the briars and mosquitoes so I wouldn't have to think, filling the bucket in less than an hour.

I left it by the side of the ditch in a cradle made by an oak that branched into several trunks and I ran down through the woods to the big flat rock, half expecting to find Bottles there, even though I knew he was still somewhere out West. I hauled myself up the steep side and sprawled out on the top, sweat stinging in the briar scratches. A hawk was going in slow circles far above me. I watched it and waited for the feeling about last night to go away, wanting things to slide back into place as they had done on the rock other times.

I kept seeing Elaine. For a second or two she would be looking at me, then she would begin to shatter into parts. And Bottles, a little drunk, was peering at the two of us, putting X's on the parts.

I sat up and began picking briars and burrs out of my clothes, trying not to see anything else. "Maybe," I said, "it should be on the third ultimate." I looked out over the valley and yelled. "That's where it should say 'Beyond here there be tigers!' "

The echoes kept yelling tigers, tigers, tigers, but when I stood up and looked down into the meadow, nothing was there.

I slid down off the rock, ran back through the woods, picked up the bucket, ran home and handed the berries to Mom.

She stared at me. "Good heavens! What happened?"

"I had to fight for the berries."

"Fight for them?"

"Yes. With the mosquitoes and briars."

She frowned at me, looking worried, and I was pleased about that.

"Steve?"

"Yeah."

She went on looking at me and finally said "I don't know," just the way Elaine said it sometimes and then always said what she really wanted to say. "Don't forget we're around if you want to talk about anything."

"I know."

I got out of there and climbed way up into the pine tree in the front yard. Talk? Tell her about last night? Try to convince Dad it had been a logical thing to do? It was as unthinkable as giving them daily reports on the big argument at high school last year about whether or not Catholic priests have penises.

A letter came from Bottles next day. Except it wasn't a letter at all, just a poem.

> Even in summer,
> When evenings are cool,
> A leg, with the dress lifted free,
> Goes pebbly with goose pimples
> Until it warms and smooths
> Under your touch.
>
> We are boys
> Wanting to be men,
> And a hand, moving along a girl's leg,
> Finds the shortest distance
> Between two places.

I read the poem standing beside the mailbox, staying there so long that Mom came to the door and called, "Is anything wrong?"

"No. Just something from Bottles."

"Oh, what does he say?"

I folded the poem and put it in my pocket. "Nothing."

She looked at me for a moment. "All right."

I whirled and ran out along the ridge to the south, all the way to the hilltop over the deep valley. I tore up the poem and let the wind take the pieces, scattering them into the dried grass of the hillside. It didn't do any good. I remembered the words.

All week, Mom kept watching me and I kept escaping. I stayed out along the road every evening after taking the cows to night pasture, watching while the brown-eyed Susans lost their color and only the white of the campions and pale blue chickory were still there in the fading light. I would go into the woods, run until I couldn't think, then drop to the ground in a clearing, looking up at the stars, counting those inside a ring around the moon to see in how many days it might rain.

I listened to all the night sounds, the gnawing, scraping, chewing, creeping and sometimes a scream as something got caught by something bigger. There were cars moving on far-off roads, dogs barking, someone calling a lost cow, the lonely sound of a one-engine plane crawling across the sky, steering along the series of beacons that flashed on the horizon.

On Saturday night I stayed along the road as usual after taking the cows out, and when Lars and Erik came by in the car, they saw me and stopped.

"You sure you don't want to go to town?"

"We'll wait while you change."

"I guess not, thanks."

I watched the car head toward Three Corners, then ran down into the valley to the schoolhouse. I wound the clock again and listened to its slow ticking before I left and climbed the steep hillside beyond the road. A car without a muffler was roaring up the valley. I could hear it for a long time before I saw it, knowing exactly where it was by the sound, getting louder on the upgrades, softening and backfiring at curves, settling into a smoother roar on the straight stretches. I remembered that a man who worked on the farm one summer always had cars without mufflers and raised a big cloud of dust because he bent the exhaust pipes down to point at the road. That was about all I remembered except that he chewed wintergreen-flavored gum and that I must have been very young then, because he had come into the dining room once after morning chores and found me getting dressed behind the heating stove. He reached inside my long johns, gave me a tweak, winked and said, "Hey, wasn't sure you had one."

The car came into sight below me, lights dimming to a deep yellow when it slowed for the turn, then blazing out white as the engine roared again. I couldn't see what kind it was, but something about the way it went roaring through the night made me think it was going straight on to California, and I wanted to race down the hill and get a ride, run away with whomever it was and never come back because everything was happening faster than I could figure out how I was supposed to feel.

23

C hurch was early because there was going to be a picnic afterwards with a ballgame and horseshoe pitching. When the service was over, I asked Dad if I could have the car and be back by the end of the picnic.

"Why?"

"Something important."

He was ready to say no. Then he looked at Mom and she thought about it a moment and nodded.

"All right," he said. "But you be careful."

They watched me leave and I started off slowly, making sure to come to a full stop at the intersection.

It was the first time Elaine had not been in the yard to meet me. I went to the door and could see a blond head through the screen. It wasn't Elaine. I didn't know how I had expected her mother to look. Somebody plain and quiet maybe, but she was just an older version of Elaine with the same blue eyes and smile.

"I'm Steve Carlson."

"Yes. Hello, Steve."

"Is Elaine here?"

She looked startled. "Why no. I thought she told you. She's gone to stay with her aunt."

"Where?"

"In Madison."

That was a hundred miles away. It might just as well have been a thousand.

"When will she be back?"

"I don't know. Maybe not until Christmas."

I stared at her.

"She's going to high school there. Her aunt — that's my sister — she's been asking her for a long time. You see, they don't have any children. . . ."

My God, I thought, she's trying to make it easier for me.

". . . and Elaine finally decided she'd like to do that this year."

"Could I have her address?"

She hesitated and I wondered how much she knew about us. Then she smiled Elaine's smile and said, "Yes, I think you could have her address."

She wrote it down and handed it to me, looking at me closely as though she was thinking the same thing I was, how strange it was that we hadn't seen each other before, just as my mother had never seen Elaine even though I was sure they would have liked each other.

I shifted back and forth in the open screendoor. "Would you tell her I said hello?"

"All right."

I had to get out of there because in a minute I was going to start crying. I petted the dog when he thumped the path with his tail, and drove on to Gordon's Landing. The Oldest Man in the World was sitting in his usual chair. I hadn't seen him for quite awhile.

"Hello, Boy. Where you been?"

"Chasing girls."

"You catch any?"

"Sure. Lost them again though, just like you."

"Well by God, you come the right day anyhow. Kind of weather makes me think I'm going to live forever, die tomorrow all the same time."

For the first time, I looked around me. The sky was a deep blue, with a cool wind blowing, lots of yellow leaves and even some fringes of red on the hillside above town.

The old man had pushed his way up out of his chair and was staring at me.

"I know," I said. "You'd like to take a drive out to Sand Creek."

He nodded.

"All right. I've got the car."

When we turned off the river road, the old man started shaking his head.

"What's the matter?"

"Was thinking of that horse of mine. He'd make that turn without me saying a word. Seemed to know just where a girl lived. You suppose every girl's got a different smell? That damn horse knew some other things, too. When I'd get busy in the buggy, he'd go nice and easy, then speed up right to the minute when I was ready to go again."

The Oldest Man in the World sat up straight on the seat as we got close, just the way he had on our last trip, then took about five minutes to get into the woods, sit down and lean back against the big walnut tree.

While I cleaned the spring, I could hear him humming some tune I didn't know. Pretty soon he began to sing, if that's what you would call it.

"When I was young'n in my prime
I was chasing a girl all the time.
I'd hug and kiss'er to start the fun,
Get me another one when I was done.
So if you find some girl who still loves me,
Just tell her I'm young as I used to be.
Yes, tell her I'm young as I used to be."

When the spring was running clear, I brought him a drink in the rusty can. He got a pint bottle of whisky out of his pocket and took a drink of that, washing it down with the cold water.

"By God! I near forgot how those two go with each other."

The can was dripping water down onto his legs, but he didn't seem to notice. It reminded me of the way Dad would go on working with flies crawling around on his hands. I never understood how he could do that.

"You know how some dogs are sight-runners, some smell-runners? Had a hound once was a sight-runner. Possum would curl up right in front of him. He'd just sniff it like it was dead, go on looking. Let anything run, he'd chase it 'til he couldn't stand up.

"Used to see some of them girls I'd had my way with, all settled down with somebody. Gave me the willies to find one of 'em looking at me. Made me want to go up to her and say 'Hey, what happened to that girl looked like you? The one I chased in the woods, us half covered with all them red and yellow leaves at the end?'

"You suppose I was the only one ever got her alive? If I'd been the one that married her, would she've up and died on me, too? Hell, I don't know. I sure do miss 'em."

"I thought you lost interest the minute you caught one."

He tipped up the bottle. "I know I said that. That's how it was, too, with a lot of 'em. Not a girl at all, just a warm place at the end of a chase. A man gets all heated up when he chases something. If it's another man, you hit him. If it's a deer, you shoot it. If it's a girl, just one thing to do, get your shot at her same as with a deer. Wasn't the meat you was chasing the deer for, though."

"Then what the hell was it for?"

"I don't know. Just did it. That's what a man was supposed to do."

He handed me the tin can and laughed. "Maybe we just couldn't stand the thought of all them unbred females running loose."

I got him more water. He poured some of it in with the whisky until the bottle was almost full again.

"There. Sure do hate to see a bottle getting empty."

"Well, what about the girl who lived here?"

He laughed. "Think you caught me, don't you? I'll admit some was different. I walked away from them, too. It wasn't just them. Hell, it was me."

He shook the bottle and let the white go back to a pale amber before he took a drink.

"I ever tell you I was a school teacher once? It was 'cause I was the biggest. Used to let half the boys out at noon to check their traps.

"I guess a time comes when you just say piss on it. It ain't going to happen. Either I missed some chance I didn't even know I had or it was all made up right from the start. So I stood in front of that solemn-faced son of a bitch of a preacher, my guts dropping out of me to think of settling down. God, she's been dead so long I can't remember what she looked like. Remember her name. Was Jessie. We said them words and went home and died."

He took another drink. "Maybe we didn't. Maybe seemed that way 'cause I spent half my days remembering how I chased them warm ones. Maybe we was even happy. Don't remember not being. Just don't remember the sun shining all the time and every day something new to chase, the way I grew up thinking it would always be. Seems like whatever was supposed to happen to me didn't happen. All I got's bits and pieces come back when the lilacs bloom, when the sun shines that certain way on a girl's hair making it a different color. Or one turns just so, maybe knowing what she's doing, maybe not, and she sticks out against cloth that's just an arm's length away. All kinds of things they do that says reach for me.

You reach all right and hell, she's just some ordinary woman like anybody else."

I refilled the can. It was for me this time. I was surprised to find the sun was shining.

When I went back to the tree, he was looking up at the hills. "Remember one year this fellow and me'd come down those bluffs on a rope, looking for caves. Found some Indian pots. Not the Indians we killed off. Older ones. Maybe the ones built those mounds shaped like snakes and birds.

"By God, some of them girls was prettier'n a brand new buggy with red-striped wheels. Don't suppose their own kids ever saw 'em that way. Can a girl you chase through the leaves one fall ever be the same one that a year later's changing a baby, the stink of that on her, all tired out and sharp-tongued, clothes not starched and pretty anymore? Are all those girls in there at once?"

He was staring at me, but I could tell he didn't expect an answer. I thought of Mom, straightening up in the garden, apron half black at the hips where she'd been wiping dirt off her hands. Or standing at the wood range, sweating, hair coming loose and getting in her eyes so she had to keep pushing it away, maybe with the back of a hand that had a fork or stirring spoon in it. That was the everyday part of her. The rest was only glimpses. The way she looked when she was all dressed-up to go out someplace. The pictures we had of her when she was young. Could that other girl, who had become my mother, ever come back?

The Oldest Man in the World was still staring straight through me, the almost empty bottle sticking up between his legs. For the first time, I realized how alone he was and felt sorry for him. Then I remembered Billy saying we were going to be the oldest men in the world someday, and I began feeling sorry for me, too.

"If it was a good life, I sure as hell never told her. Why didn't I wait one more year, I'd say to myself. If I'd gone to one more dance. If I'd just walked up to a certain door, why this girl would be standing there, maybe drying her hands on her apron. We'd've stood smiling our fool heads off, both knowing we'd finally found each other. Well, that never happened, maybe 'cause you got to pay for things, one way or another, so I got married. Hell, she was a good enough woman all right. Took good care of me. My mother died on the trail, coming up from Ohio, right after I was born. But damn it to hell, I didn't want a good woman. I wanted. . . ."

He took a deep breath, emptied the bottle and put it back into his pocket. He was looking at me again, and now he was seeing me. For a minute I thought he might really tell me what I'd been trying to find out all summer.

"Hell, I don't know what I wanted. Know what I want now. Want that spunky one to come walking out through a door that ain't there. With a wild look and hair back over one shoulder like she's already running. And barefoot. She was always barefoot."

"Couldn't you ask somebody what her name was?"

"Now just who the hell do you think there is left to ask?"

I went over to the spring and stayed there, feeling foolish. When I looked at the old man, his eyes were closed. I had a notion to go and kick him awake. I wanted him to say, "Son, I been talking about me. Now let's talk about you. Seems like you're all mixed up about girls. What is it you're trying to figure out?"

Even if he had said that, I wouldn't have known what to tell him, except maybe to say, "I want the same thing you do. I want to get my shot at them, like deer hunting. And I want to be with them on the top of some hill, just talk with them and know they're somebody, instead of seeing just legs and hips and breasts without a face most of the time. Except I don't mean *them*. I mean Elaine."

I ran over and stood right above him. "That's what I want!" I yelled. "Damn you, I want you to tell me which way it's supposed to be!"

The can of cold water was in my hand. I dumped it right on to his face. He groaned a little, but didn't even open his eyes. I backed away, sat down on the old foundation and realized I was crying.

Every now and then the old man's lips moved and little sounds came out, the same thing over and over. At first I couldn't tell. The sounds went on and it seemed like a name. It could have been Marta. Then it was clearer and I was pretty sure he was saying "Martha."

He stopped that after a few minutes. I couldn't even see him breathing. I nudged him and nothing happened. I had to shake him for quite awhile before he woke up. He ran his hands across his lips and looked at me. "You know the worst thing about being old?"

I shook my head.

"It's having your mouth leak when you sleep. Waking up, finding your pillow wet with spit. That's the worst thing."

He looked at the ruins, his eyes only half open. "What season is it, Boy?"

"End of summer."

"Thought for a minute spring might be coming. You sure it's not early spring?"

"I'm sure."

"Well. Be a long time before the lilacs bloom. Always figured that's when I'd remember."

I almost told him then, but he was still staring at the old foundation, and not thinking of anything except himself again. He didn't even know I was there.

I had to put my arm around him to get him back to the car. I did the same thing getting him into his chair at the station, and wondered if people were watching, thinking I took the Oldest Man in the World out and got him drunk.

When I drove down to the end of the street to turn north on the river road, I saw the warden's wife standing at the edge of the river, beyond the little shack where Eva Mae and I had been way back at the beginning of summer.

I stopped the car and watched. It was the first time I had seen her since the day on the bluffs. She was all dressed up this time, as though she had been to church earlier, with a white blouse and bright blue skirt, hair braided and pulled into coils on top of her head. She looked older with her hair that way and I might have driven on except that she started skipping rocks on the smooth water of the river. Then I went over to her.

She threw. The rock skipped seven or eight times, leaving little spreading ripples that curved downstream in the slow current.

"You're pretty good at that."

She jumped, pulled her blouse straight, then laughed. "Oh, it's you. Hello. Steve, is it?"

"Yes."

"You ever find that girl?"

"I met somebody else."

She laughed. "Have you lost her yet?"

"I guess so. It's been that kind of summer."

"Oh. I'm sorry."

She still had a flat rock and was tossing it back and forth from hand to hand, looking a little embarrassed when she noticed what she was doing.

"Might as well use it," I said.

She did, bending down low, throwing underhand with a full sweep of her arm, the stone going way out and skipping more times than I could count. She stayed in a half-crouch as she watched it, her body twisted, pushing against her clothes and I could see the bulge just below her waist for a moment before she straightened up again.

I stared at her because I hadn't thought of her as anyone that grown-up before. Her faced turned a little red as though she knew I had noticed.

"I've been wanting to tell you. . . ." I said. "I mean, there's something. . . ."

I could feel my own face getting red. "That place up on top the bluffs. There's somebody who knows about that."

"Oh. Was it you who blew the horn that day?"

"Yes."

"Was somebody else there, too?"

"Yes."

"Thank you, Steve."

I looked beyond her, out over the river, watching the brown water move steadily to the south.

I heard her take a deep breath. "I guess you think. . . ."

I remembered them on the hillside, the sound of their laughing, the way she ran and her hair flying, a picture out of a fairy-tale book. I remembered crying when books like that ended, not because the stories were finished, but because I didn't want to lose people who had become part of me.

"No," I said.

I noticed the freckles. They made her seem younger again. "You were . . ." I had to force myself to say the word I had probably never spoken out loud before, "beautiful."

I was afraid for a minute she was going to give me a hug right there, but she only smiled.

I started to go, then turned back because it wasn't enough just to remember her as the warden's wife.

"I don't know your name."

"It's Elizabeth. Mostly, everybody calls me Beth, but I like Elizabeth."

I left, getting back to Three Corners just as the picnic was ending. Dad walked around the car, whistling, pretending not to notice while he carefully checked to see if I had hit anything.

24

I wrote to Elaine and took the letter with me on the first day of school, mailing it from Three Corners so no one at home would know.

Billy was standing at the front school door, watching everybody coming in. He kept shaking his head.

"What's going on?" I asked.

"Hell, they're the kind of girls could find a rubber in your pocket, blow it up and ask whose birthday party you been to. How come they all look ten years younger than me?"

"Because you already found out you're going to be the oldest man in the world someday. You didn't know that when school started last year."

He looked at me for the first time. "What the hell's the matter with you?"

"I guess I'm in between girls again."

"Jesus," Billy said, "it's not the end of the world."

"Well it's the end of something, all right."

"Then I got just the thing for you, Steve. You can join me and Pete's club."

"What kind of club?"

"Six-pack-a-day club. We're going to keep a little glow on and not even know we're here."

"I'm already not here," I said.

There were a few new kids in my class and some of the old ones were gone. Spring was already back in another world. I was lucky to find out if somebody missing had died, moved away or just dropped out.

Lars pulled me aside after chores one morning, putting his arm on my shoulder the way he'd been doing now and then when he was feeling like a parent.

"Steve, they been all over the country looking for Harvey Shields. The sheriff was in the tavern asking if anybody knew anything. I told him about you seeing Harvey that night. He might want to talk to you."

I pulled away. "You're going to get me in trouble with Dad."

He nodded. "Maybe. It seemed like it might be important."

On Saturday the sheriff's car came bumping out across the hayfield where Dad and I were fixing fence. The sheriff was a big-bellied man. He hadn't walked more than two hundred feet, but he was already puffing when he came up to the fence. He shook hands with Dad, then turned to me. "You Steve?"

I nodded.

Dad was looking at me as if he had never seen me before. My God, I thought, he's wondering if I robbed a bank or maybe got somebody pregnant.

"Seems your son here saw Harvey Shields just before he took off."

"That right?" Dad said to me.

"Yes."

"You should have told us."

"I didn't know it was important."

The sheriff leaned against the last post we had put in. "Son, we don't know what's become of him. What you tell us could be mighty helpful. Now where was it you saw him?"

"At the bridge. Just up the valley from his house." I saw Dad start thinking about that.

"What time was it?"

"After midnight, I guess."

"What did it seem like he was doing out there that time of night?"

"He was just standing there by the bridge," I said.

"And you saw him and stopped?"

"Yes, I stopped."

"You know," Dad said, "we've talked about that road. I asked you boys not to use it."

"It's safe at night. You can see the lights if anybody's coming."

"Be even safer if you were walking."

The sheriff cleared his throat. I kept watching the post he was leaning on. It was already tilting. I hoped he would lean on it harder and it would dump him.

"That's all he was doing?" the sheriff said. "Just standing there?"

He was looking for something, I almost said. Don't you know the Goddamned night's full of people wandering around looking for things, not even knowing if it's for something they lost somewhere or something they still haven't found?

"Well, he was drinking. I remember he threw the empty bottle over into the ditch. I guess you could find the pieces."

The sheriff wrote in a little notebook, stopping every couple of words to lick the end of the pencil.

"Did he say anything to you?"

Hell yes, a lot of things, I wanted to say. About my mother and about his bald head and about a girl who went away, up to Minnesota.

"He talked about how he'd spent all his life taking care of his mother."

The sheriff put his notebook away and buttoned the flap pocket of his shirt. "You ask me, he drove in the river someplace. We'll find him someday."

He started to go, then turned. "You sure it was the night before he left you saw him?"

"I'm sure. There was a full moon." And I told Harvey I caught the girl I'd been chasing, but I didn't tell him her name was Elaine who said then she was never going to change.

The sheriff puffed his way back to the car. Right away I fixed up the post he had been leaning on. I didn't want to talk about it with Dad, but he surprised me, just started pounding in staples. Except for Lars and Erik teasing about the sheriff coming to get me, no one said another word.

For the next few weeks I waited, afraid they would find him in the river or in some dark, narrow hollow, so filled with brush that even hunters didn't go there. No one found him. I began to believe he really had gone looking for that girl with eyes the color of wild asters and, whether he found her or not, had started over again someplace.

The dry weather went right on into October and Elaine didn't answer my letter. I wandered in the woods whenever I could, waiting for something to happen. Sometimes I sat for a long time on a hilltop, watching the season change, the tall, dry grass singing in the wind, red and yellow leaves rattling past me, blowing off the ridge and sailing out over the valley, some of them falling, some whirling away out of sight.

Sometimes I tried to think the summer back to life, remembering everything I could about the girl at High Ridge, then Anne, then Elaine, and they kept moving away from me until I couldn't even see them.

Sometimes at night I ran down the hill to the schoolhouse, low-hanging white oak branches, still covered with brown leaves, scratching at me. I would stop the clock, set it at exactly midnight, then race back along the hillsides that were silent now because the whippoorwills were gone and frost had killed the katydids.

Once I hitched a ride to Gordon's Landing to see Billy. For a change the Oldest Man in the World wasn't out front.

"He's in bed," Billy said. "Been there a week." He waved me through the door. "Go say hello."

I had never been inside before, but all I had to do to find the Oldest Man in the World was follow the smell of his pipe. He was propped up on three pillows in a little bedroom that had yellow wallpaper with wild roses on it. There were no books or pictures, not even a calendar.

He never gave me a chance to say anything.

"Hello, Boy. I'll be getting up out of here soon as winter's over." He poked at me with the pipestem and winked. "We can go fishing again."

Then he started telling about the buffalo and wolves on Elm Tree Island. I waited until he went to sleep and left him.

Billy sneaked four cans of beer out of the cooler and we hopped a north-bound freight, riding on top this time, the wind cold, but the top of the boxcar gathering and holding some of the sun's warmth.

Billy laughed when we went by Elm Springs and pointed toward the river. The clammer was out there cranking up his chains. "Who we looking for this time?" Billy said.

I didn't know who I was looking for. Maybe Elaine, except the train didn't go to Madison and I didn't think she would want to see me anyway. If she wanted to see me, she wouldn't have gone away in the first place.

"I guess I'm not looking for anybody," I said. "It was the best thing I could think of next to getting hold of a car and driving to California."

"We could get a car," Billy said. "Fishermen don't take the keys out half the time."

"Not and drive all the way to California we couldn't."

The sun went under the clouds and we just about froze to death for the last ten miles below La Crosse. We got off there and started wandering around. No matter what we were looking for, it wasn't any use. Maybe because of the cold wind, the place looked as if it had been abandoned.

"My God, I think I'm about to get a case of the screaming blue willies," Billy said. He took off on his own and went aboard a towboat.

I walked on the campus of the college, kicking a path through the leaves, waiting in the shadowed afternoon under the bare elm trees for something that never came. Maybe for Elaine to appear by magic and be waiting for me, realizing what she had lost. Maybe for a long-haired girl I had never seen before to drive up in a convertible, take one look at me and say, "Get in."

Billy found me there, sitting with my back against one of the big trees. I had been crying. When I saw him coming, I started throwing leaves up in the air, letting the wind carry them off, hoping he wouldn't notice. He sat down with me, carefully not looking as he handed me a beer.

"What the hell?" he said. "Screw Elaine!"

"It didn't help," I muttered. I remembered Bottles saying he'd given up girls because he couldn't stand the loneliness.

"Damnit, Steve! None of 'em are worth getting all twisted up about. Who the hell does she think she is, anyway?" His voice was rough and he patted me awkwardly on the shoulder. The idea of Billy feeling sad for me made me want to start crying all over again.

"It's Anne, too," I said, feeling too mixed up to tell him the rest. I had started out feeling bad about Elaine, all right, but in the middle of it I began thinking about Anne and that was what I had been crying about when Billy came back.

He was crumbling up leaves, his face all twisted. "Anne's the only one you can't lose and might even find again because you didn't ever get a chance to find her in the first place."

I started laughing. That was the longest sentence I had ever heard from Billy. It sounded as if he had been thinking it up for about a year and as if there might be a Bottles part of him in there just waiting to get out.

"Want to look for Anne some more?" he asked.

"No!"

"Why not?"

I went on laughing because at least it was better than crying. "We might find her. Then, according to you, I'd lose her for sure."

"You're crazy," Billy said, but he suddenly looked very pleased with himself.

25

Willy and Marge got married in late October. On that same day the wind started blowing hard out of the northeast, growing steadily colder, by late afternoon bringing with it a driving rain that knocked down the last of the red leaves.

"Good Lord, I think it's going to snow," Dad said when we came out of the barn after evening chores.

The three of them went on toward the milkhouse, walking side by side, carrying the two ten-gallon cans of milk between them. I watched them, remembering how Lars and Erik and I used to fight about whose turn it was to be in the middle and have to help lift both cans.

The rain was rattling against the tin roof of the silo, the wind howling under the leaves. I could see my breath in the lantern-light. I closed the barn door and stood staring at the light. When had we started using lanterns again? Summer still seemed to be hanging over me with nothing ended and suddenly it was fall with Dad talking about snow and the shortest day of the year only two months away.

I drove alone to the big old white church that stood all by itself out in the country, getting there in time to work in the rain with two other boys on Willy's car. Then, bringing a wet wool smell with us, we went inside to see it happen.

Marge was still just distant and smiling in her white dress, Willy red-faced and sweating the way he always was when he was with her. He fumbled around for what seemed like ten minutes getting the ring on her finger. I tried imagining it was Elaine and me in front of the preacher, with the whole world looking at us and knowing what we would be doing before the night was over. It didn't work; it was just Willy and Marge up there.

When I got to Willy in the handshaking line, he leaned close and winked. "Tonight for sure," he whispered.

"Yeah. You finally made it."

He kept holding onto my hand, his face screwed up, about ready to cry. "I'm sure going to miss you. By God, I'll never forget that night of the cows long as I live."

"The best thing about that night was you telling Marge to shut up."

He didn't seem to hear me. He was still pumping my hand up and down. We said goodbye as though we had been good friends and would never see each other again.

The rain had changed to snow when we followed Willy and Marge out of the church and threw rice as they got in the car and drove off, towing the line of tin cans we had tied to the rear bumper. There were chains on the front tires and rocks tumbling in all four hubcaps. The two boys who had helped do that watched the car go.

"Well, tonight he has a piece of paper says it's legal."

"How does he know she's got one?"

"He touched it once."

"The hell he did!"

"Yeah. He told me. She went to sleep in the car. He managed to touch it."

"Was it cold?"

"What do you mean, cold?"

"I mean was it cold like something made out of marble?"

I didn't understand why I was feeling as though I was losing something important. I started for home, the big flakes of snow swooping up over the windshield. Then I remembered it was Saturday night and I cut off through the hills toward Indian Springs.

Jake didn't see me come in, so I played "It Makes No Difference Now" on the jukebox and waited to see what he would do. It had hardly started before his head come up and he gave me a big smile.

"Hey, Steve! Where you been lately?" He looked around. "Where's that girl? Where's Elaine?"

"Summer ended."

"Aw, hell. I sure liked how you two looked together. Any chance of patching it up?"

"I guess not."

He put a beer down in front of me. "She was something, all right. But what the hell? There's others. I'll even drink to that."

He raised his glass and moved along the bar. "A toast, you sad bastards! To the ones we've lost and the ones waiting in line!" He drained his drink without taking a breath. A few of the others drank with him.

Jake came back to me, shaking his head. "God, but it's a sorry night in here. Still snowing?"

I nodded.

"Well to listen to the talk you'd think it was going to be ten feet deep by morning. Hey, Steve, remember I been keeping track what songs get played on my jukeboxes? Well, guess how it worked for love songs, unsuccessful."

"Maybe half."

"Wrong. Eighty-six percent! What you figure that means?"

"I guess people've got a lot to feel sad about."

"Or maybe they like to feel sad whether they have anything to feel sad about or not."

"Yeah. Or maybe some of both."

"Anyway," Jake said, "I figure sad people drink more. So the more sad music I put on the jukebox the more booze I sell." He slapped me on the shoulder and set up a round of drinks on the house. "Here you go, you bastards. Now let's have a little action in here."

I sipped my beer and listened to the talk.

"Yes, sir, going to be a bad one, all right. Had any sense we'd be heading south with the birds."

"Damnit!" Jake said. "You all forgot about squaw winter? Get one just about every year. In a few days the sun'll be out and you'll all be complaining about the heat."

"What about those duck hunters got froze to death that year out in the Mississippi bottoms? You call that a squaw winter?"

"Hell, that was the middle of November."

"No, it wasn't. It was Armistice day. The eleventh."

"Are you going to call me a liar over four lousy days?"

"Sure I am."

"Hell," Jake said. "I only lie about important things."

The man laughed. "I believe that, all right. Hey, Jake, remember that girl lived up on Beaver Creek? Used to ride horses a lot?"

"Sure," another man said. "Went galloping around singing her head off. Bareback, too, more often than not."

Jake was looking from one man to the other, not moving, one hand holding a glass under the beer spigot, the other on the lever.

"Well," the first man said, "you know she married somebody from out in the Nebraska Sandhills. Met at a rodeo over in Iowa, I think."

"What about her?" Jake said.

"Just heard today. She got thrown off a horse a month or so back. She died out there."

Jake still hadn't moved.

"Hey, Jake, didn't you used to have something going with her?"

"That was a long time ago."

"Then why you standing there like somebody just kicked you?"

Jake pulled the lever and filled the glass. "She was somebody special, that's all." He smiled. "Any time I was with her, just seemed like I was going to live forever." He put the glass of beer down and stared at it.

"Sure sounds like you still had a thing for her."

Jake whirled around. He grabbed the man's shirt. "Goddamnit! You don't listen! It's got nothing to do with her."

He pulled the man along the bar by the shirt, poked a five dollar bill in his hand and shoved him out. "Here! Get drunk someplace else!"

Jake slammed the door and came back to the bar.

The door opened and the man stuck his head in. He looked about ready to cry. "Can I come back tomorrow?"

"Oh, for Christ sake, get in here. Just shut up, that's all."

The man climbed onto a barstool. "Do I have to give the five dollars back?"

"I said shut up!"

"In that case, the drinks are on me."

There was a burst of laughter and the talk started again.

I went out. The snow was finer now, glowing around the street lamps, beginning to blow along the sidewalk. The gusty wind half covered the sound of music from the dancehall across the street.

I bought a ticket and stood in a dark corner, watching. It wasn't more than a couple of minutes before I saw Elaine, her face against somebody's shoulder. The couple turned. It was Bottles with her. They were dancing slowly and close together like some idiot couple about ready to go steady. I had never seen Bottles dance before. I watched them for quite awhile. He was a little clumsy, but there was something so damned gentle and careful in the way he held her that I wanted to punch him in the nose. The music stopped. Bottles looked up and saw me just as I was ducking out.

I went back across the street to Jake's. He took a quick look at me and shook his head. "I guess you just saw a ghost."

"She's over there. Elaine is. With Bottles."

Jake nodded. "I guess that figures. Girls go for guys like him. Something romantic as hell about them. I lost a girl to a guy like that one time. You know when I stopped thinking about her? It wasn't when they got married. Hell, you can always make up ways she could get out of that and come back to you. When she got pregnant was when I really stopped thinking about her."

He opened up the jukebox and pushed some buttons. "There, it'll run all night playing nothing but love, unsuccessful." He put another beer down in front of me and let me alone.

In a few minutes, Bottles came in and sat on the barstool next to me. I slid one of my beers over to him. We didn't look at each other and I took quite awhile to tear a very neat hole in the middle of my bottle label.

"How's Tools?" I said.

"He joined the army."

"What the hell for?"

"To be a mechanic. They've got lots of trucks and things. He'll be all right."

"What about Girls?"

"I don't know, but I think he's probably all right."

"What do you mean, you don't know?"

"He still never came back from that night of the excursion steamer. Wherever he is, I guess we know what he's doing."

I remembered when I first knew them, how they were always a threesome. "Well, for Christ sake!"

Bottles laughed. "You know what happened? It was that damn car. We sold it to get some money and that was the end of us."

"I got your poem. You really going to college?"

"Yeah."

"What's it like?"

"Different."

"How different?"

"Very different."

"Aw, come on, Bottles! Different, how?"

He poured his beer and forgot to stop. The foam came up and sloshed over the side of the glass. It was the way he used to do when he was drunk. I looked at him for the first time. He wasn't drunk. He was just staring, straight ahead.

"I don't call myself that anymore."

"What the hell do you call yourself, then?"

"You're going to laugh. Harold."

"*Harold?* That was somebody named *Harold* sitting in the Hole in the Wall? That was *Harold* talking about the game of X's?"

"I said you'd laugh."

"The Hole in the Wall burned down! Did you know that? It's just three concrete steps leading into a weedpatch now! Did you know that?"

"No, I didn't know that." He lifted his beer. "To three concrete steps and a weed patch, a fitting monument for somebody named Bottles."

He filled his glass too full again and for a moment he was who he used to be. "Hell, Steve, it's just like trying out for a high school play. I wanted a different role for a change."

"Well for Christ sake! Is there still a Bottles in there someplace?"

"Of course. Sometimes being Bottles is the only way I keep from crying all the time."

He started to pat me on the shoulder, then pulled his hand back. "Good old Steve. Still a good old straight, wandering around backstage, everybody else assigned a part by now. Don't you know you got to play somebody you can hide in? Don't you even know yet you got to act older than you are or the Goddamned world'll just pass you right by?"

"Bottles, I don't know what you're talking about."

"Course not. Don't even know who you're listening to. It's not Bottles talking. It's Harold talking."

"Well then, damnit! Harold doesn't make any more sense than Bottles!"

"I know. That's what I'm telling you. Trying to make sense is what causes all the touble."

The jukebox was playing the song that said "I can laugh about it now, but sometimes I still want to cry."

"What about Elaine?" I said.

"She'd like to see you."

"All right."

I got up and left some money for the beer, surprised to find there still were other people in the bar and the place filled with voices. We went outside into the snow and started toward the dancehall. In the middle of the street I stopped and Bottles, or Harold, or who the hell ever he was, bumped into me.

"Wait a minute. Does she want to *see* me? Or want to say hello?"

He shifted back and forth. The snow was creaking under our feet, our breath making white clouds.

"I guess say hello."

"You two got something going?"

He nodded. "Maybe."

"You checking over the used statues?" I said. "You hitting them on the foot, finding one that's alive?"

"She spoke my name," he said.

"Yeah. She spoke mine, too! I guess you could say she's my X-girlfriend. She speak your name before or after you poked her ultimate with yours?"

He shook his head. I realized his hair was cut shorter. It wasn't flying all over the place, but of course this was Harold's hair.

"I sent her a poem, too. She wrote to me. Anyway, I thought it was all over with you two."

"Sure. All over. Like you used to say, or like that fellow Bottles used to say, 'It makes no difference now.' "

He put out his hand. "Thank you for the beer. I mostly nowadays prefer brandy. That seems more fitting for Harold."

I didn't take his hand. He looked at it hanging out there between us and laughed. It was the first time I had ever seen him look awkward.

I went back to the bar, each step creaking so loud in the snow that there were echoes. At the door, I turned. He was still standing in the middle of the street, looking about four feet tall and ten years younger than the Bottles who had gone West to follow the harvest only three months ago.

"For Christ sake!" I yelled. "You're going to get run over!"

He still just stood there.

I walked back and stopped in front of him. "Tell her. . . . Tell her I forgive her for everything I did to her. Tell her, sometimes I still want to cry. Oh, hell, just tell her I miss her."

"All right. I'll tell her."

He was looking very small again. "Bottles," I said. "For Christ sake, Bottles."

I couldn't leave him that way. I put my arm around his shoulders and gave him a hug. He smiled. I watched while he walked to the dancehall and went inside.

26

For a week the cold, blustery weather went on, a mixture of snow and rain falling, the snow coating the ground occasionally, then melting from the stored warmth of summer. I re-read old books from the attic, almost wanting it to be real winter, that dead time of year when everyone stayed closer to home and I wouldn't have to think about anything.

But it wasn't winter. One night the old dream came back, the girl running away, just out of reach, along the creek. For a moment the light was too dim for me to see the swinging hair as anything except a shape. She moved into the moonlight and I could tell she was not blond. The hair was dark, the way it had always been, and even in the dream I knew it had all been dreamed before. This time the girl was not laughing when she turned to look over her shoulder. And she was so real and close I woke up half out of bed, reaching for her.

"Steve!" Mom was calling. "Steve, are you all right?"

"Yeah."

"You were calling something over and over."

"It was just a dream."

"Is there somebody named Anne?"

I got back into bed and didn't answer. At least I still knew her name. But when I tried to remember the dream I couldn't be sure anymore. Maybe Billy had been wrong. Maybe I had found Anne enough so that I could lose her. Maybe it had been the same darkhaired girl who was always there in the dream and she was the only one I had left.

Next morning while I was walking to school, the sun broke through the dark, scudding clouds and was suddenly warm against my back. Bright green grass was sticking up through the patches of melting snow. The wind, blowing gently from the southwest, was filled with the smell of wet leaves, asters, and frost-browned goldenrod.

While I stood watching summer come back again, the sound of the grade school bell echoed up the ravine from the valley. I thought of the clock ticking slowly away, all the kids held captive at their desks on a day like this, and what I wanted to do was get my horse and gallop down into the valley, head pulled inside my sweater so I would look like a mysterious headless horseman, and I would run in, turn the clock ahead to four, then run out again, leaving behind a screaming teacher and a room full of frightened, staring faces as I galloped away.

I walked on to high school.

Billy was waiting for me. "Let's drink our lunch in the barn."

"What do you mean, drink it?"

"Sure. I got two six-packs stashed in a bucket of ice."

"I don't believe it."

"You'll see."

When I went out at noon, there was blue haze on the horizon in every direction. Billy had the beer, all right. He and Pete were already started on it in the old empty barn across the fence from school.

"I think," Pete said, opening another bottle, "This is what you call drinking on an empty stomach."

"That's only for the first one," Billy said.

"How you figure?"

"After the first one you're drinking on a stomach that's already got beer in it."

Billy laughed and handed me a bottle. "Hey, guess who's going to have a baby."

"Not Willy and Marge already?"

"Nope. The game warden's wife."

"I knew that a long time ago."

Billy looked disappointed, and I told them about the day I found her skipping rocks.

"She sure was a pretty girl," Pete said.

"Yeah," Billy said. "She sure was."

They were both talking about her as though she had died. The boards inside the barn were still dark along the cracks from the rain and snow. There was a smell in the place of old moldy hay and all the livestock that had come and gone.

"What ever happened to Flora?" I said to Billy.

"Who's Flora?"

"You know. Girl you had at High Ridge, around the end of May."

He tipped up his beer. "Hell, who can remember that far back?"

I could. There was something funny about me remembering somebody he'd already forgotten.

"She was fat. You took her to French Prairie, with a bunch of guys in an old Chrysler."

"I still don't remember." He smiled. "For that matter, what happened to the one you found at High Ridge?"

"She got away."

"Yup. You was always losing one girl back then while you was chasing you another one."

"What about Elaine?" Pete said. "I was the one you took her away from, remember."

"I didn't take her away. You passed out is all."

"What happened to her anyway?"

"I let her get away, too."

"Boy, she was something," Pete said. "You ever get into that?"

He was looking at me, expecting every little detail. "I don't want to talk about Elaine." I opened another bottle.

"I still think she's got a hell of a nerve doing this to anybody like you," Billy said.

"What do you mean, anybody like me?"

"You know."

"No I don't."

"Yes you do. You think I'm so stupid I don't know you play in a different league than me?"

Pete blinked at Billy. "Hey, I thought you made out all the time."

"Sure. And they're all slobs. I wouldn't know how to make out with somebody that's got class if you gave her Spanish fly and put her in bed with me."

I stared at him, remembering how he had been making me feel about ten years old only a few months back. "Billy, I don't know what the hell you're talking about."

"You wouldn't." He opened another beer. "Here. Let's get to important things. This talk's giving me the dismals."

We worked away at the beer. Pete was rocking back and forth on an old milkstool. Billy was staring at the wall, his face all twisted up so I knew something was coming.

"I think she was too old for you," he said.

"What're you talking about? I'm older than she is."

"Yeah, but girls are born older right from the start."

His face was still that way.

"What's the matter with you?" I said.

"I don't know. Yes I do. I just been thinking. There's a whole 'nother summer coming next year that we got to get smart enough to make it through without wrecking a car, getting arrested or knocking anybody up."

All at once I was angry and felt like crying at the same time. "You want to know something?" I yelled. "We're not going to get any smarter! We're just going to get older! We're going to wear different clothes and hope everybody will think we're smarter! You know something else? I haven't met a son of a bitch yet who knows what to do after he catches up with a girl he's chasing!"

"Everybody knows what to do when you catch one," Pete said.

"Yeah, but do you know what to do after you do what you do when you catch one?"

Pete shook his head. "That doesn't make any sense, what you just said."

"That's because you've had three beers."

"Five," Billy said. "He's on his fifth. I've had four. You've only had two."

"Which just shows to go you," Pete said.

By the time we finished the beer, Pete was asleep. We left him in the barn and went back to school where about twenty people told us the principal had been looking for Billy. He had his coat on when he came back from the office.

"What's going on?" I asked him.

"They're coming to take me home."

"Did something happen?"

"I don't know. They just said be ready."

Billy looked back from the door. "Hell, I guess nothing could happen to somebody who's already the Oldest Man in the World."

"Hey," I said, "when you see him, tell him. . . ."

Billy waited.

"Never mind. I'll tell him myself sometime."

During a late afternoon free period, I was half asleep from the beer and went to the back of the room and pushed up a window. The wind had gone around even more to the south, a warm, soft wind. I leaned out, letting it get at me, and for some reason I was seeing Elaine sitting beside the fire, turned orange by the flames, at our picnic on Green Cloud Hill.

A hand came down on my shoulder. Old Miss Corning started leading me back to my seat, her fingers hooked in deep.

"Everybody remembers things when Indian Summer comes," I said and got ready to duck.

She just looked at me. Finally she let go of my shoulder and patted me on the arm. "There, there. Tomorrow's Saturday."

She walked back to the front of the room, her thin ankles and baggy stockings flopping around in her high heeled shoes, the way they always did. It was the first time I had thought about her being young once and knowing anything about the feel of seasons changing.

27

*A*ll morning Dad had been quietly singing his Norwegian songs. He was still singing after breakfast when he went to check the field across the road from the house. None of us knew what the words of the songs meant. The only way we could tell anything was by watching his face. He came back smiling a little, but his mind off somewhere else, and said the ground was still too wet for fall plowing.

"Damnit! It's not fall!" I wanted to yell. "It's summer again!"

He sent Lars and Erik out with shovels to check for new ditches in the fields, and he and I worked together at the granary, filling bags with oats and loading them into the car. I opened the barnyard gate for him and he headed for town to get the oats ground at the mill.

I was raking up leaves in the yard when he came back. He stopped and stood looking at me, a funny expression on his face, before going on into the house.

In a few minutes Mom called me. Dad was sitting at the table drinking coffee.

"Sit down a minute, Steve." She looked at me the way she always did when she was trying to decide how to say something. All I could think of was that somebody had found out about the beer yesterday.

"Would you like to try some coffee? I'll put lots of cream in it."

"What's the matter?" I said.

"Did you hear anything about Bill Wallin yesterday?"

"Just that Billy had to go home."

"Well, you know he'd been sick."

"Sure. I saw him a few weeks ago. He told me about the buffalo and the wolves, except this time it was only two wolves. He said he was going to get up pretty soon."

"He was right about that," Dad said.

At first I thought he was joking, but he wasn't smiling.

"What happened to him?"

"He got up sometime yesterday morning, walked away without anybody seeing him. They still haven't found him."

Mom put her hand on my arm. "Remember it's been since yesterday."

"I know where he is," I said.

Dad's head snapped up. "Where?"

"Sitting under a big walnut tree up on Sand Creek."

They looked at each other, at me, then at each other again, so startled I almost laughed.

"Are you sure?" Mom said.

"I'm sure. At least that's where he'd try to go."

"Why would he do that?"

"Because the weather changed yesterday. He probably thinks it's spring. He thinks the lilacs are about to bloom."

They waited.

"He knew somebody who lived there once."

They looked at each other again. Dad took a deep breath and let it out. "If you figure that's where he might be, we need to show them."

I thought of the roaring cars, flashing lights and sirens screaming. "Not with all the others."

I could see Dad thinking about that. "I tell you what. How about we go down there, just you and me, and see?"

"All right."

We drove the ten miles without either of us saying anything, but several times I could feel him looking at me with all the questions he wanted to ask so he could get everything neatened up.

There were a lot of cars around the station in Gordon's Landing and a siren blowing somewhere to the north. We drove right on through and Dad turned onto the Sand Creek road without my telling him. I showed him where to pull to the side and park. For a minute he looked at me, frowning, because from the road there was no way of telling there had ever been a house back there. I pointed to the top of the walnut tree, sticking up above the other timber.

Dad stopped me when I started to get out. He was only gone a few minutes. He got back in the car and put his hand on my shoulder. "He's there all right. He's dead, Steve."

Dad started the car.

"I want to see him."

He turned off the engine. "All right."

He was leaning back against the tree, maybe slid down a little more, but otherwise no different than the other times when he had just been asleep. I had thought he would be fallen over or something. His pocket bottle and the rusty tin can were on the ground beside him. When I leaned down to look at his face, he was the same as ever. I couldn't tell if he had remembered. I checked the spring and there was a place cleaned out and clear water running into the pond. At least he hadn't died in bed, like somebody old.

I went back and looked at him again. I wasn't angry at him anymore and I was sorry I hadn't told him.

"I think her name was Martha," I said.

I went back to the car. Dad turned it around and headed for Gordon's Landing.

"Maybe that's the fourth ultimate. But shouldn't something happen in between three and four?"

I didn't know I had said any of it out loud until Dad frowned at me. "Son, I guess I don't know what you're saying."

"I don't either. Dad, do you think people's lives pass in front of them when they die?"

"I don't know, Steve."

He parked across the street from the station. "You wait here." He started to go over there, then came back. "They'll be asking how you knew."

"I drove him out there a couple of times."

Dad nodded. I watched him cross the street and begin talking to the group of men. I could tell when he said where, because they all looked down-river. He talked some more and they all looked across the street at me. One man moved toward the car. Dad stepped in front of him and talked some more. In a few minutes they all got into cars and roared out, leaving the town empty. I didn't see Billy anywhere.

Mom was waiting for us on the porch. Dad told her what had happened. She took my arm, led me inside and sat me down at the table.

My God, I thought. Now we're all going to have another cup of coffee and talk about it.

Sure enough, she filled my cup and they sat there waiting for me to say something.

"Did anybody at the station know who used to live out there?" I asked.

"Good Lord, no. They didn't even remember a house ever being there. Son, I don't suppose anybody's lived at that place since back in the 1800s."

I felt myself getting stubborn. "Don't forget, he was the Oldest Man in the World."

They looked at each other.

"He knew who lived there, all right," I said. "He just couldn't remember. I think it's been more than seventy years."

They watched me and waited.

"It was a girl he knew out there. He lost her someway. He used to talk about it at the station."

"Then why on earth didn't anyone think of looking there?"

"Because they didn't listen to him anymore, that's why. He couldn't remember what her name was. He thought if he went out there he might remember."

Dad leaned back. He had an odd, almost sad expression. "Well, maybe there's some value in not having life last forever."

Mom gave him one of her question looks.

"I mean because we can get stuck someplace."

He looked at me again. "You liked old Bill, didn't you?"

"Sure."

"I think he was stuck someplace. Like a puppy that never stops chasing its tail."

I wanted to argue with him, but I got tangled up in trying to decide if he meant anything special by the word "tail."

He tilted back in his chair, nodding. My hands were pushing me up out of my seat. I wanted to yell at him. I wanted to push him over backwards. He was trying to make everything into some definite kind of meaning the way he always did. He couldn't seem to see that a lot of things just have a certain feel to them and you don't have to understand what they mean to know they are something you don't want to lose.

I jumped up and jerked the leather suitcase out from under the couch. Right on top there was a picture of him when he was about twenty, his arm around a girl in a white dress. I grabbed it and slapped it down in front of him.

"All right! What about the time you spent with her? Did it mean anything you can explain? Did it get to be all neat and logical? Or did you just do it without knowing anything except you had to do it?"

I was shaking. Mom pulled me down into my chair.

"Well?" she said, looking at him.

He picked up the picture and stared at it for a long time. He even turned it over and looked at the other side, but there was no help there. "I don't even remember who she was."

"Her name was Belle," Mom said.

"That's right. I guess it was Belle. How'd you know that?"

"I know about a lot of things." She put her hand on his arm. "So somewhere there's a forty-year old woman you may have been in love with when she was a young girl. Is that so strange?"

He put his hand over hers and it was one of those moments when I had no place in what they were thinking.

I still wanted to yell at him. I couldn't. I wanted to say, "For God sake, try to remember you were young. Then maybe we could talk about it. Maybe even talk about Elaine who belongs to somebody named Harold now. Or talk about how, for the rest of my life, I will never drive by Elm Springs without wondering what happened to Anne. Or how someday I'm going to be the oldest man in the world, saying 'You know, it's a funny thing, I never even knew that first girl's name.' "

He suddenly turned and looked at me, almost hearing me, but all we did was sit and stare at each other.

Finally he shook his head. "I guess looking back doesn't do any good either."

I didn't even know if he meant that for me or for Mom.

He reached toward me. If he patted me on the head I knew I was going to push him right out of his chair. His hand came down on my shoulder. I left it there a minute, then slipped out from under him and ran outside into the sunshine.

I saw the leaves I had raked up. I made a flying leap into the pile, pulling the leaves over me, but even hidden that way I was seeing the Oldest Man in the World as a puppy who was chasing his own tail and the girl coming out of that house to laugh at him.

I sat up, heaping the leaves around me so only my head stuck out, knowing before I saw them, they were going to be on the porch, side by side, watching me.

"I'm sorry I tried to tell you! You're too old to remember!"

They stood there, American Gothic, not saying anything.

"All you need is a cameo and a pitchfork!"

They stood there.

"I knew her name and I didn't tell him!"

It was the way it had been lately. They didn't hear a word I wasn't saying. Mom smiled a little, maybe remembering something of her own that had nothing to do with me. Dad was frowning, the way he always did when I worried him and he looked inside me to see what needed fixing. I could see him running different thoughts past himself, one by one, while he tried to understand. I remembered the way he had stepped in front of the man in Gordon's Landing who was starting across the street toward me. I wanted to thank him.

I couldn't do that.

I jumped up, leaves flying. Using my arms like brooms, I swept the leaves together again on the bare ground of the path, scratched a match and set them on fire. The flames moved up quickly, blue smoke swirling around me, hiding the porch.

I started running, through the brown grass of the yard, into the pale green of the hayfield, the smell of burning leaves clinging to me, saying it was no use pretending summer had not ended.

At the edge of the woods I stopped and looked back. They were still side by side on the porch, looking after me through the blue smoke that was rising straight up into the blue sky.

I waved to them.

Her hand came up first, arm stretched full-length. Then his, in a careful, head-high wave.

I turned and ran again, into the hiding shadows of the woods, down into the deep hollow, and up onto the flat rock where I could see everything and be seen by no one. So I could watch the valley below for something to happen in the meadow where nothing ever happened unless I wanted it to. So I could look up into the narrow hollow, toward the old well-casing where there must have been a house once, and wonder if those people had ever learned anything about themselves. So I could turn my mind off and just feel the sun's warmth and the roughness of stone under me, smell the damp soil and old leaves, hear birds singing, bees working the flowers.

I did that, as I had always done since I was first old enough to be in the woods alone, whenever I had lost something.

This time it was not the same. Even if I was still just seventeen, I had already found out there is no use looking in distance, or anywhere else, for what is lost in time. I didn't want to know that. I didn't want to see what I was seeing in the empty meadow down below.

THE EMPTY MEADOW

ILLUSTRATED AND DESIGNED BY MARIAN LEFEBVRE
EDITED BY DOUG BRADLEY
TYPESET BY TOTAL TYPE IN BASKERVILLE
PRINTED, SMYTH SEWN AND BOUND BY WORZALLA PUBLISHING COMPANY
THE TEXT PAPER IS GLATFELTER OFFSET
THE ENDPAPER IS MULTICOLOR ANTIQUE/WILLOW GREEN
THE COVER CLOTH IS ARRESTOX BY JOANNA WESTERN MILLS

THE EMPTY MEADOW
WAS PRODUCED BY
STANTON & LEE PUBLISHERS, INC.
UNDER THE DIRECTION OF
MARK E. LEFEBVRE, EDITOR-IN-CHIEF,
WHO ACQUIRED THE MANUSCRIPT

*B*en Logan — novelist, non-fiction writer, lecturer, producer/writer of films and television — lives in two separate worlds. While he pursues his livelihood in New York City, another part of him remains rooted in the southwestern Wisconsin hill country of his childhood. In his earlier, award-winning book, *The Land Remembers,* Logan speaks of forever belonging to that land, "even though I have been a wanderer."

In *The Empty Meadow,* Logan has again come home to his Wisconsin world, creating a community of sharply-etched characters who are, in his words, "captives of a time, a place, and a way of thinking about what is supposed to happen between the sexes."

Logan is married to Jacqueline Stoner of Mexico City and is the father of three children. He and his family live 40 miles north of New York City in a house built in the 1690s.

*M*arian Lefebvre, illustrator and designer, is best known for her illustrations in the *We Were Children Then* books. One critic commented that these illustrations "are like the memories of the writers, distorted somewhat by the years, romanticized a little by imaginations that seek to love the past, yet full enough to bring reality to what might be thought of as a dream." In her art, she continually recreates the past, both in mood and historical detail.

She is also an award-winning designer, most notably for *The Only Place We Live.*

FICTION   G98515 $14.95

Logan, Ben, 1920-
The empty meadow.